"Adeline Waugh's food has caught my eye from day one. Her recipes are incredibly delicious, unique, and truly some of the most stunning food I have ever had."
—**RACHEL MANSFIELD**, author of *Just the Good Stuff* and creator of *rachLmansfield.com*

"Adeline Waugh makes clean eating an art form with her vivid colors and her beautiful, holistic ingredients. Her recipes and photography are a joy for the senses and the taste buds."
—**SHIVA ROSE**, author of *Whole Beauty* and creator of holistic lifestyle website, The Local Rose

"*Vibrant & Pure* is filled with whole-food–based anti-inflammatory recipes, and is as beautiful as can be! Adeline's mission is to share how changing one's diet can make a huge difference in one's personal healing journey. This book is a true staple for anyone on a wellness path of their own."
—**LAUREL GALLUCCI**, CEO & Co-founder Sweet Laurel

"Packed with food styling tips, advice for stocking a whole foods kitchen, and stunning, approachable recipes, *Vibrant & Pure* is a must-have book for anyone looking to make simple, nourishing food that's also a feast for the eyes."
—**JEANINE DONOFRIO**, author of *Love & Lemons Every Day* and *The Love & Lemons Cookbook*

"*Vibrant & Pure* is filled with inventive flavor combinations and innovative uses for produce that will make even proclaimed veggie-haters salivate. This is the type of book that will re-ignite excitement about cooking and redefine how delicious healthy food can be."
—**LIZ MOODY**, host of the *Healthier Together* podcast and author of *Healthier Together*

"*Vibrant & Pure* is an absolute delight for the senses. This book is a work of nutrient-dense art and I cannot wait to test out the recipes in my kitchen!"
—**NITSA CITRINE**, creative director of Sun Potion Transformational Foods

healthful
recipes
for bright,
nourishing
meals

VIBRANT & PURE

ADELINE WAUGH

Clarkson Potter/Publishers

New York

Published in the United States by Clarkson Potter/Publishers, an imprint
of Random House, a division of Penguin Random House LLC, New York.
clarksonpotter.com

CLARKSON POTTER is a trademark and POTTER with colophon is a
registered trademark of Penguin Random House LLC.

Library of Congress Cataloging-in-Publication Data

ISBN 978-0-525-57509-2
Ebook ISBN 978-0-525-57510-8

Printed in China

Book design by Stephanie Huntwork
Cover and interior photography by Adeline Waugh

10 9 8 7 6 5 4 3 2 1

First Edition

contents

introduction

Ever since I was a little girl, I've had a burning desire to be creative. I never imagined what form that creativity would end up taking or how I would express that feeling until five years ago when, as a last-ditch effort to help heal my skin, I realized I needed to overhaul my eating habits.

You're probably wondering what I mean by that. What could I have been eating that was so bad? Let me paint a picture for you. Like most college students, I was downing two to three energy drinks per day to stay awake longer, all the while eating disturbing amounts of fast food during study breaks. I was truly the picture of *un*-health. I had never given even a cursory glance at a nutrition label, nor thought twice about the obvious connection between how tired and unhappy I felt and the food I was eating. I've always had a fast metabolism, so I never thought I had to worry about my diet. The late-night pizza and excess drinking definitely led to some weight gain, but not enough for it to be a big concern of mine. My skin, on the other hand, was worse than it had ever been. I have suffered from cystic hormonal acne since I was fourteen years old. I'm not talking about your run-of-the-mill, puberty-induced breakouts. I'm talking unrelenting, deep carbuncles covering my entire face, neck, chest, and back, leaving long-lasting scars, pain, and embarrassment. You'd never catch me without pounds of makeup on my face. I tried absolutely everything to get rid of my acne, from topical solutions to prescription medications. Nothing worked.

When I was twenty-five, a few years out of college, I came across an online article discussing the connection between diet and acne, and suddenly that relationship clicked for me. I began reading books on the topic and researching incessantly—and I changed my relationship with food almost instantly. I began to read ingredient lists on packaged foods; for the first time I noticed if something was organic, non-GMO, and most importantly, nutritious. I started cutting out all of the processed stuff and focused on eating *real* foods that came from the earth. I greatly reduced my intake

of refined sugars, dairy, and gluten to see what I might be sensitive to. The results were pretty miraculous. Not only did my skin clear up and actually begin to glow but also my whole body felt *incredible*. I was hooked on real, unprocessed food and this new healthy lifestyle. I felt an overall improvement in my state of well-being; the anxiety, irritability, moodiness, and brain fog all decreased. Though it wasn't my main goal, I even ended up losing nearly 20 pounds simply by cutting out all the inflammatory foods. I had never felt so confident in my own skin, literally. It was as if my body were screaming, "THANK YOU!" for finally giving it the nutrients it needed to function properly.

Now here's something I never thought I'd say: I am grateful for my acne because it's what brought me to this place. I launched an Instagram account called @vibrantandpure to document my journey to health and to share the meals I was creating. I quickly realized my passion wasn't just creating inventive, healthy meals; it was also in making food look as beautiful as it was nutritious. That was because I began to focus intensely on food styling. I'd go to sleep thinking about ways to combine flavors, how best to present them, and what colors (all natural, of course) went best together. I'd wake up and jump out of bed, ready to execute those ideas. The most thrilling part was that people really started to take notice.

A few years later, after developing and honing a unique style, and even starting some major food trends, I still wake up every morning excited to create and share my recipes with the world. *Vibrant & Pure* is a food experience for your mouth and your eyes.

how to build a vibrant kitchen

Here you will find all the tools, ingredients, and pantry essentials you will need to use this book to its fullest potential.

EQUIPMENT

juicer

Juicing of any kind is good for your health, but I highly recommend a cold-press, auger-style, or masticating juicer, as it squeezes out juice from your greens and vegetables without heating them, so no nutrients are killed during the process. Perhaps the best part of using one of these juicers is that you can leave the skin on anything you want to juice—as long as you wash it first, of course.

high-speed blender or bullet

I own a Vitamix, but there are so many other great high-speed blender options out there. This is one of my most-used kitchen tools, and I would probably be lost without it. If you're looking for a more economical option, try a bullet juicer!

food processor

I use my food processor to make sauces, dressings, marinades, and even to mix some batters for baking. Depending on the size of your food processor, you may have to mix some ingredients in two batches.

ice cream maker

If you want the option to consume delicious dairy-free ice cream and be able to control the type of sweetener and other ingredients that go in it, you'll need one of these.

nut-milk bag

If you're a nut for nondairy milk, I recommend making your own at home. That's not only because it tastes way better than the store-bought stuff but also because you can control exactly what goes in it. So much of the nondairy milk you find at the store is loaded with additives and preservatives. The bags you need to make nut milk can be purchased online or in most natural foods stores. My favorite homemade nondairy milks are almond, cashew, hazelnut, hemp seed, and pumpkin seed.

INGREDIENTS

VIBRANT PANTRY

I make a point of using organic protein and sugar-free condiments whenever I can, so it's my hope that you will, too!

bread

For all my toast recipes, feel free to use your favorite kind of bread. I typically opt for a gluten-free sourdough or oat bread, but the recipes can all be enjoyed with whatever floats your boat.

SPROUTED If you don't have a gluten sensitivity and you find that your body handles the gluten in wheat and some other flours, well, then sprouted breads, like Ezekiel bread, are a great option.

FERMENTED Another bread option is one that's made with a naturally fermented starter, like sourdough bread. Fermented breads are often easier on the digestive system. If you can find a gluten-free sourdough bread, that's even better!

GLUTEN-FREE I try to use gluten-free bread 99 percent of the time because I've found that it's less inflammatory to my skin. When choosing a gluten-free bread, I recommend either making your own (bonus points!) or finding a brand at the store or online that uses the fewest ingredients possible (I recommend Barely Bread which can be found online). Lots of foods slap on the "gluten-free" label and are mistaken for health food when they are truly anything but. If you see 25 ingredients listed that you've never heard of, avoid the bread.

eggs

All my recipes use large, pasture-raised (when possible) eggs. Be aware that labels on egg cartons can be misleading; for instance, "cage-free" means the hens weren't kept in cages, but it doesn't mean their communal living conditions are good. Opting for "pasture-raised" ensures that you're getting not only the most nutritious eggs but also hormone- and antibiotic-free eggs. If you're vegan, or just not into regular eggs, try baking and cooking with a Chia Egg (see page 152).

oils and healthy fats

Quality fats are essential to our health. Not only do they help us absorb nutrients, but they make healthy food more delicious. These are my favorite fats and oils to cook with; take note of the best ways to use them in your kitchen!

avocado oil (for high-heat cooking)
extra-virgin olive oil (for low-heat cooking, drizzling on vegetables, or in salad dressings)
grass-fed butter (for high-heat cooking)
grass-fed ghee (clarified butter; for high-heat cooking)
toasted sesame oil (for dressings and sauces)
unrefined coconut oil (for high-heat cooking)
veganaise or avocado-oil mayonnaise (for dressings and sauces)

acids

When I feel there is something missing from a recipe, I add a dash of acid and it instantly brightens the dish. Acids are necessary for balancing strong flavor profiles like salty, sweet, and fatty.

apple cider vinegar
lemons
limes
red wine vinegar
rice vinegar
white wine vinegar

condiments and seasonings

cayenne
coconut sugar
crushed red pepper flakes
Dijon mustard
fish sauce
maple syrup
pink Himalayan sea salt
pomegranate molasses
raw honey or manuka honey
sriracha
tamari (gluten-free soy sauce)

PRETTY POWDERS AND SUPERFOODS

CHLOROPHYLL DROPS Chlorophyll is the green stuff in plants that's oh so good for you. You can get this in its pure form to drop into your water or into your dairy-free cream cheese for Mermaid Toast (see page 135). It can be found at most natural foods stores or online.

SPIRULINA AND BLUE MAJIK Spirulina, and its more colorful cousin blue majik, might just be the super-est of all superfoods. It's often touted as the most nutrient-dense ingredient on the planet, a type of blue-green algae that boasts so many health benefits (anti-cancer and cholesterol-lowering, as well as reducing chance of a stroke, to name a few) and happens also to be loaded with protein. I also love it for its deep greenish-blue color, making the perfect shade for Unicorn Toast (see page 132). Spirulina and blue majik can both be found at most health-food stores or online.

BEE POLLEN Bee pollen is a complete protein that's rich in minerals, enzymes, vitamins, antioxidants, and amino acids. It's great for the immune system, and it just so happens to be one of my favorite forms of healthy decoration. Think of it as yellow sprinkles that are *really* good for you.

TURMERIC Turmeric can be used in savory and sweet dishes alike, so I throw it into everything so as to benefit from its anti-inflammatory properties at every opportunity. The active chemical in turmeric is an antioxidant called curcumin; our bodies best absorb the curcumin when turmeric is consumed in combination with black pepper and a healthy fat.

NUTRITIONAL YEAST Nutritional yeast is a form of deactivated yeast that's loaded with B-complex vitamins and minerals. It has an amazingly cheesy, umami flavor that's tasty on salads and popcorn.

COLLAGEN PEPTIDES Collagen peptides are a bio-available form of collagen, which is the stuff responsible for keeping your skin firm and your bones and joints healthy. They are a great addition to any smoothie, matcha tea, or coffee drink because they are flavorless, but packed with benefits. Collagen peptides are available at most health-food stores or online.

styling

Food styling is a skill that can be for everyone—the home entertainer wanting to wow their guests by adding a touch of magic and whimsy; the parent trying to get their child to eat healthy foods (beets don't seem so scary when they're hidden in bright pink milk); and the curious home cook who wants to to try something new and develop a more fun relationship with food. Styling is where I find my own creativity really has a chance to shine.

eating with your eyes

The concept of food styling may seem foreign or even frivolous to the uninitiated. Playing with food and producing something beautiful is by no means a necessity, but it facilitates creative expression and it's fun! Beyond that, learning to style your meals can improve a distorted relationship with food; it gets you thinking about the limitless possibilities of what can be eaten, how to create it, and beautiful ways to display it, rather than the more typical dialogue that revolves around deprivation and limitation.

Don't believe the stereotypes about healthy food being boring. It's quite the contrary. Healthy foods, as in unprocessed and pure foods, are not only the most beautiful to look at, but also taste the best and make us feel the best. The more colorful and deeply pigmented a food is, the healthier it is for you. Using a variety of colors in each meal ensures you're getting a wider variety of vitamins. This is why we're told to "eat the rainbow"—the more colors you can get on your plate, the better!

basic guidelines for composing a dish

1 Use Color and Color Variation

Beyond contributing to your health, using a variety of colors is essential to successful food styling. When arranging an Instagram-able dish, I use basic complementary colors—that is, orange with blue, pink and red with green, purple with yellow, and so on. Check out the Ingredient Palette (see below) for a list of foods organized by color! I'm not saying you need to be concocting rainbow bagels and unicorn milkshakes on the daily. What I'm saying is that a meal with no color is never going to wow you—and chances are, it won't be all that healthy either.

AN EXAMPLE: a bowl of plain brown rice isn't that appealing to look at, and it can only do so much for your nutrition. But once you start adding toppings like a bright green sauce made from fresh herbs and immunity-boosting garlic, slices of bold pink watermelon radish, and chunks of bright-purple sweet potato, you've not only created an eye-catching meal but you've also ensured your body is getting the nutrients it needs: chlorophyll from the green herbs, vitamins and minerals from the radish, and vitamin A from the sweet potato.

2 Use Texture and Shape Variation

Texture and shape can totally transform a dish both visually and taste-wise.

AN EXAMPLE: if you're serving something smooth, like hummus, add a crunchy topping like roasted chickpeas or mix in something with precise edges, like chopped carrots. It's amazing how the small additions you make to contrast the textures visually almost always equally improve the taste and experience of eating the dish.

3 Don't overdo it

When it comes to styling, less is often more. Now, this is simply my personal preference; I'm not here to dull anyone's sparkle or tell you how to play with your food. In my experience, it is best to stick with a few colors and textures in each dish. For example, if you have a piece of toast with every color of the rainbow and every shape and texture, it will look a little too busy and overwhelming.

Always keep the contents of your plate smaller than the plate itself, so the food doesn't appear crowded.

INGREDIENT PALETTE

These are my favorite ingredients, organized by color, so you can plan to eat with your eyes as well as your mouth.

red
strawberries
chiles
blood oranges
raspberries
pomegranate seeds

orange
peaches
papayas
carrots
apricots
oranges

yellow
passionfruit
mangos
acorn or
kabocha squash
lemons
bananas

green
avocados
matcha tea
greens and
microgreens
cucumbers
peppers
kiwi

blue/violet

radicchio
eggplant
blueberries
blackberries
purple cauliflower

pink

watermelon radish
grapefruit
beets
watermelon

my eating principles

"Eating healthy" means different things to different people. For me, all the noise surrounding diet and food went away when I realized "healthy" could mean just getting back to food basics. That's how I operate, and that's how I develop recipes. Of course, there is room for indulgences and exceptions, but the key to eating well is to simply eat foods that come from the earth and that are not processed or packaged. When I cut out gluten, dairy, and refined sugar to cure my acne, I naturally started gravitating toward more nutrient-abundant foods like fresh fruits and vegetables.

Almost all the recipes in this book are free of gluten, dairy, and refined sugars because, beyond eating as much fresh, organic produce as humanly possible, you'll find those are the three other principles of eating for your skin and health. If you follow these guidelines to a tee, I'm confident you will start to look and feel better than you ever have before. But, of course, don't hesitate to adapt these guidelines to fit your lifestyle and choose which work best for you—after all, every person is different.

1 **Skip the conventional dairy.** Most cow's milk is inflammatory and we actually have no dietary need for it. Dairy is often one of the first ingredients people struggling with acne are advised to remove from their diet. After a few months of experimenting with eliminating dairy, I saw leaps and bounds of improvement in my acne and my digestion. I sometimes eat raw goat or sheep's milk cheese because I've found that I don't experience those negative side effects, and in the same vein, grass-fed butter and ghee are also okay. As a rule, though, the less dairy, the better.

2 **Avoid gluten.** Gluten, a natural protein found in wheat, barley, rye, and a few other grains (and in our favorite carbs like bread, pizza, and pasta), was one of the first things I cut out on my health journey, and it made such a huge impact for me. I quickly felt less bloated, my skin started to clear up, I lost weight, and I felt more energetic. Unless you are eating freshly milled wheat and grains, you are likely ingesting some gut- and skin-irritating chemicals used to process wheat for conventional, mass produced flour. Even if you don't have celiac disease or a gluten sensitivity or intolerance, cutting out gluten could be the answer you didn't even know you were looking for.

3 **Cut out refined sugars.** Refined sugars (found in most sweets and canned and packaged goods) used to rule my life. When they are part of your diet, you constantly crave more sugars, taking you on a blood sugar roller-coaster. Sugar sources that haven't been heavily processed or refined, like raw honey, maple syrup, or coconut sugar, don't have such a heavy glycemic load and won't wreak havoc on your skin and overall health.

4 **Opt for organic foods.** Standard supermarket produce can come from genetically modified plants, sprayed with toxic pesticides, and grown with petroleum-based or sewage-sludge fertilizers, so, obviously, it comes with hazards. I like to take back as much control as I can from the food industry and buy organic. Crops grown organically in the United States have to be raised without those aforementioned nasty things; organically grown livestock must have access to the outdoors, be given organic feed, and be antibiotic- and hormone-free. Not only is this healthier for you, but it's also better for the environment!

With *Vibrant & Pure*, I invite you to shift your perspective and view cooking as an opportunity to experiment with new flavors and textures that will feed your body, soul, and creative spirit. When you begin to focus on how good it feels to add bright, beautifully-hued ingredients to your diet, you won't stress over getting rid of the foods that don't serve you. I want you to feel your best, and I know firsthand that this is possible through the magic of food. Eliminating potentially inflammatory ingredients while moving along on your health journey can seem daunting in a culture that is so obsessed with dieting and restricting foods, so my goal is to make this a positive experience that you'll crave and turn into a lifestyle.

I want to ensure that you never equate eating healthy with deprivation or boredom. Think of this book as your greatest tool for starting a fresh and rewarding journey with food. Healthy food can feed your body *and* your soul. Once you get your kitchen and pantry stocked with these vibrant foods, you can begin creating beautifully delicious meals and start *thriving*.

smoothies, shakes, and juices

pb and j shake

Take a hop and a skip down memory lane and indulge in this homage to the peanut butter and jelly sandwich. Whether you enjoyed yours crustless or au natural, with crunchy or creamy PB, or with store-bought jelly or your grandmother's homemade preserves, PB and J sandwiches were the crème de la crème of childhood. This nondairy shake combines natural peanut butter (none of that sugar-laden stuff here!) and real fruit to deliver that beloved flavor combination. Add your favorite vanilla-flavored protein powder to make it a clean and super satiating protein shake.

1 cup frozen strawberries

1 banana, fresh or frozen (about 1 cup sliced)

1 heaping tablespoon natural peanut butter or peanut butter powder

1 tablespoon chia seeds

½ cup nondairy milk

½ teaspoon ground cinnamon

1 scoop vanilla protein powder (optional)

Place the strawberries, banana, peanut butter, chia seeds, nondairy milk, cinnamon, and protein powder (if using) in a blender, and blend on high until fully combined. Add ½ cup water or more nondairy milk to thin, as needed.

collagen almond butter shake

SERVES *1*

Raise your hand if you love peanut butter cups. Now raise your other hand if you also want healthy, firm skin. Are you sitting there with both of your hands raised? Time to make this fiber-rich and healthy fat-filled shake. Coconut meat is a great way to bulk up your shakes and keep you full for hours. Beyond being sweet, dates are also an amazing source of fiber and magnesium that help rev up your digestive system. As for the collagen peptides, I throw them into most of my shakes and smoothies to give my hair, skin, and nails a healthy boost. So next time you've got a hankering for some peanut butter cups, whip up this healthy, satisfying shake. Add some chocolate or vanilla protein powder if you're extra hungry or want to refuel post-workout. Pro tip: if you have more of a sweet tooth, add up to 4 dates for some extra sweetness!

½ cup frozen coconut meat or frozen banana

1 cup nondairy milk

2 pitted dates

2 tablespoons cacao powder

2 tablespoons almond butter

1 scoop collagen peptides

Pinch of kosher salt

½ cup crushed ice

1 scoop chocolate or vanilla protein powder (optional)

½ cup water

Place the coconut, nondairy milk, dates, cacao powder, almond butter, collagen peptides, salt, ice, protein powder (if using), and water in a blender, and blend on high until fully combined.

mint cacao chip smoothie

One of my favorite ways to eat spinach is when it doesn't actually taste like spinach. Raw cacao nibs, which give this smoothie a chocolate flavor and crunch, also happen to be *loaded* with precious antioxidants. Cacao nibs are basically nature's healthy chocolate chips. The fresh mint leaves and peppermint extract give the smoothie that refreshing mint taste, but if you're just using mint leaves, add extra to get more flavor. Spirulina gives this smoothie a gorgeous green hue—plus, a few extra nutrients never hurt anyone.

1 frozen banana (about 1 cup sliced)

1 cup baby spinach

¼ cup fresh mint leaves

1 tablespoon cacao nibs

¼ teaspoon peppermint extract (optional)

1 cup nondairy milk

½ teaspoon spirulina

1 or 2 pitted dates, to taste

1 cup crushed ice

Place the banana, spinach, mint leaves, cacao nibs, peppermint extract, nondairy milk, spirulina, dates, and ice in a blender, and blend on high until smooth. Add up to 1 tablespoon of water to thin, as desired.

beet rosewater sorbet smoothie bowl

SERVES *1* OR *2*

This bowl of sorbet is a breakfast treat as delicious and decadent in flavor as it is brilliant in color. Using almost exclusively frozen ingredients and minimal liquid produces a thick texture that rivals your favorite sorbet. The crunchy, aromatic Pistachio Coconut Rose Dukkah is the perfect topping (seriously, it's going to be your new obsession). Make sure you plan ahead, as you'll need to prepare the coconut-milk ice cubes ahead of time. If you're a rosewater fan, consider adding an extra ½ teaspoon to each serving.

4 ice cubes made from full-fat coconut milk

1 cup frozen raspberries

½ teaspoon rosewater

1 tablespoon chia seeds

½ cup diced peeled raw beet

2 pitted dates

1 frozen banana (about 1 cup sliced)

2 tablespoons water, plus more as needed

1 tablespoon Pistachio Coconut Rose Dukkah (recipe follows)

1 Place the ice cubes, raspberries, rosewater, chia seeds, beet, dates, banana, and water in a blender, and blend on high until smooth and thick. Add up to ½ cup water, a tablespoon or two at a time, to thin as desired.

2 Immediately spoon into bowls and top each with some Pistachio Coconut Rose Dukkah.

pistachio coconut rose dukkah MAKES ABOUT ¾ CUP

2 tablespoons shelled pistachios

2 tablespoons pumpkin seeds

2 tablespoons hazelnuts

3 tablespoons unsweetened shaved coconut

1 teaspoon fennel seeds

2 teaspoons sesame seeds

1 to 2 tablespoons dried edible rose petals, **finely chopped**

Sea salt, **to taste**

1 Either by hand or using a chopper, finely chop the pistachios, pumpkin seeds, hazelnuts, and coconut.

2 In a small skillet, toast the pistachios, pumpkin seeds, hazelnuts, coconut, fennel seeds, and sesame seeds over medium-high heat for about 3 minutes, or until the nuts and coconut start to turn a light golden brown. Let cool for 5 minutes.

3 In a small bowl, combine the toasted nuts and seeds, rose petals, and salt. Use immediately or store in an airtight container at room temperature for up to 2 months.

lemon–blueberry pie smoothie

SERVES _1_ TO _2_

If you ask me, everything should taste like pie. Blending lemon zest and blueberries with dates and warm spices like cinnamon creates a flavor mimicking pie crust with a tart filling that will change your life. I often add a scoop of my favorite vanilla protein powder and drink it for breakfast. For an extra-healthy boost, add some leafy greens (don't worry; it still tastes like dessert). For a more dessert-like experience, top the smoothie with crumbles of Chocolate Chip Cookie Dough (see page 202).

1 frozen banana (about 1 cup sliced)

⅓ cup frozen coconut meat

1 cup frozen blueberries

½ teaspoon ground cinnamon

1 teaspoon grated lemon zest

Juice of 1 small lemon (1 tablespoon)

1 pitted date

⅛ teaspoon grated nutmeg

1 cup nut milk

½ teaspoon vanilla extract

Handful of crushed ice

Place the banana, coconut, blueberries, cinnamon, lemon zest, lemon juice, date, nutmeg, nut milk, vanilla, and ice in a blender, and blend on high until smooth. Taste and adjust sweetness and tartness levels to match your preferences.

greenest smoothie

I love my green juices, but sometimes when I need a little more, I love to make a big batch of this green smoothie and keep it in the refrigerator for an energy boost later on. I use green apples because they tend to be the lowest in sugar, but feel free to use whatever variety you like. If you are worried about the "green" taste, add some ripe banana for a hint of sweetness. Trust me, before long you'll actually begin to crave that fresh "green" taste. If you're using an organic lemon (and a high-speed blender), try blending the lemon with the peel on—it adds amazing flavor and covers up any bitter flavor from the greens.

2 cups chopped fresh kale

2 celery stalks

¼ English cucumber or 2 Persian cucumbers

1 whole lemon, preferably organic

1 green apple

Place the kale, celery, cucumber, lemon, apple, and 1 cup water in a blender, and blend on high until smooth.

sunshine shot

Throwing back this shot of freshly juiced ginger, turmeric, and cayenne can be a bit jarring, but it makes for one illness-kicking potion. Not only is it loaded with immune boosters, but it also has anti-inflammatory properties. Even if I'm already sick, I find that drinking this elixir helps to decrease the time I am actually ill. As for that aggressive aftertaste? I've taken care of that with sweet, tangy pineapple—it's the perfect burn-easing chaser. Pro tip: add some minced garlic for extra cold-busting power!

2 whole lemons

3 (1-inch) pieces fresh ginger

2 (1-inch) pieces fresh turmeric

⅛ teaspoon cayenne

1 or 2 small slices fresh pineapple

Add the lemons, ginger, and turmeric to a juicer and juice according to the manufacturer's instructions. Pour into a small shot glass or two and stir in the cayenne until combined. Chase the shot with a pineapple slice.

minty green juice

I am probably caffeine's number one fan, but I am here to tell you that a quality green juice can replace even the best cup of coffee first thing in the morning. It's bursting with the energy of fresh vegetables and fruits, and the boost is immediate. The best part is that, unlike coffee, the energy that a green juice provides doesn't follow with a crash or cause dehydration; in fact, drinking these water-rich vegetables will leave you super-hydrated and buzzing from a whole bunch of good-for-you nutrients. I've added mint because it soothes indigestion, so next time your stomach feels off, or you just need a boost of natural energy, whip up this minty green juice.

1 bunch **Tuscan kale**, washed

1 cup fresh **baby spinach**

1 large **English cucumber**

6 **celery stalks**

1 cup loosely packed fresh **mint** leaves

1 **green apple**, diced

1 **lemon** (skin on), preferably organic

1 Place the kale, spinach, cucumber, celery, mint, apple, and lemon in a juicer and juice according to the manufacturer's instructions.

2 Pour into a tall glass to enjoy immediately, or store in an airtight container in the refrigerator for up to 4 days.

root juice

SERVES *1*

All the vibrant and deeply pigmented root vegetables in this sweet immune-boosting juice will paint your fingers shades of pink, red, yellow, and orange. When they say "eat the rainbow" for your health, this is definitely what they mean. Beets help to protect your liver against toxins, while turmeric and ginger provide anti-inflammatory properties. The second this potent, crimson beverage hits your lips, your body will thank you.

1 large beet, peeled

6 medium carrots

1 green apple, sliced

1 whole lemon (skin on), preferably organic

4 (1-inch) pieces fresh turmeric

1 (1-inch) piece fresh ginger

Place the beet, carrots, apple, lemon, turmeric, and ginger in a juicer and juice according to the manufacturer's instructions. Pour into a tall glass to enjoy immediately, or store in an airtight container in the refrigerator for 4 days.

fennel and pineapple juice

SERVES 1

When I first changed my diet, the extent of my fennel knowledge pretty much topped out at knowing it tastes somewhat like licorice. Now that I'm enlightened, I use it whenever I can. Not only is it delicious but it's also chock full of health benefits. Back in the day of natural medicine, fennel was often used to treat indigestion and heartburn. Pineapple contains the digestive enzyme bromelain, which helps us break down food and absorb nutrients more efficiently. So, when you take a sip of this powerhouse green juice, not only are you improving your digestion but you're also alkalizing your system with kale and lemon, hydrating your body with cucumber, and purifying your blood with parsley.

1 bunch **Tuscan kale**, washed

1 **fennel bulb**, trimmed

4 **Persian cucumbers** or 1 large **English cucumber**

1 **lemon** (skin on), preferably organic

1 bunch fresh **parsley**

2 cups cubed **pineapple**

Place the kale, fennel, cucumber, lemon, parsley, and pineapple in a juicer and juice according to the manufacturer's instructions. Pour into a tall glass to enjoy immediately, or store in an airtight container in the refrigerator for up to 4 days.

elixirs and cocktails

pink rosewater cashew milk

This dreamy pastel pink "milk" tastes as magical as it looks. Raw cashews are a great source of healthy fat, and they're also full of vitamin E, magnesium, and zinc. It's delicious in lattes and equally good on its own. Pro tip: it takes chia pudding to a whole new level. Plan ahead here, because the cashews require 6 to 12 hours of soaking.

tip: To soak nuts for milk, simply add them to a jar or bowl, and cover with water.

1 cup raw cashews, soaked and drained

1 tablespoon diced raw beet

1 teaspoon rosewater

2 tablespoons honey (preferably raw unfiltered or Manuka)

1 Place the cashews, beet, rosewater, honey, and 3 cups water in a high-speed blender, and blend on high for at least 30 seconds, or until fully combined and smooth.

2 Using a nut-milk bag, strain the contents from your blender into a medium bowl to separate the liquid from the solids. Pour the milk into glasses to enjoy immediately or store in an airtight container in the refrigerator for up to 4 days.

mermaid milk

To put it in the least scientific terms possible, chlorophyll is the stuff that makes plants green. We all know that eating lots of leafy plants is super-good for us, so supplementing with pure chlorophyll drops is a shortcut for getting that green goodness. Pouring this creamy and beautiful green elixir over some Granola Crack Clusters (see page 84) is my favorite way to feel like a magical creature at breakfast time. If you're not in the mood for a pastel green milk, omit the chlorophyll drops and enjoy this as a plain hazelnut milk. Plan ahead here, because the hazelnuts require 6 to 12 hours of soaking. (see Tip, page 46).

1 cup hazelnuts, soaked and drained

4 pitted dates

1 teaspoon ground cinnamon

1 teaspoon vanilla extract

Pinch of sea salt

1 dropper full of liquid chlorophyll or 1 teaspoon spirulina)

1 Place the hazelnuts, dates, cinnamon, vanilla, salt, chlorophyll, and 4 cups water in a high-speed blender, and blend on high for 30 seconds, or until fully combined and smooth.

2 Using a nut-milk bag, strain the contents from your blender into a medium bowl to separate the liquid from the solids. Pour the milk into glasses to enjoy immediately or store in an airtight container in the refrigerator for up to 4 days.

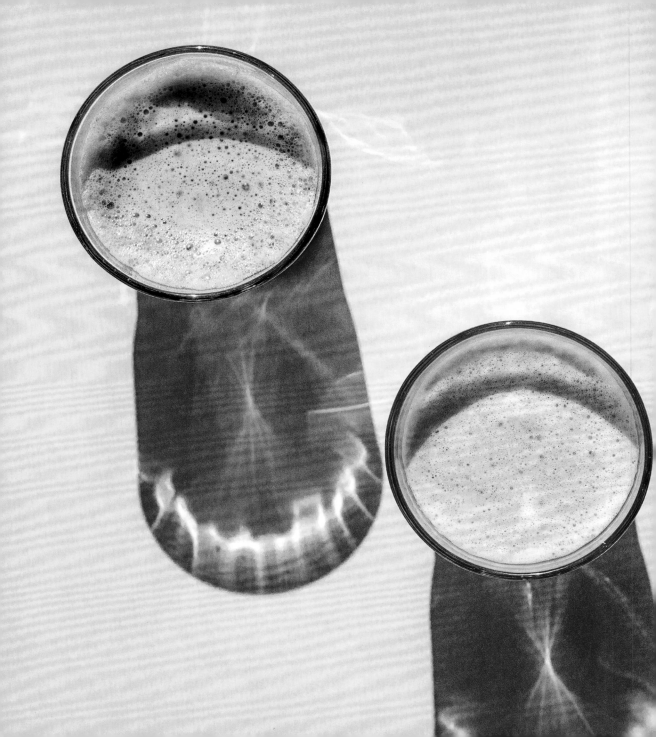

golden milk

Let's talk golden milk. This vibrant yellow beverage is loaded with many beneficial ingredients, the main one being oh-so-potent turmeric. Known around the world for its anti-inflammatory properties, turmeric has been used medicinally for centuries. This latte is viewed traditionally as a relaxing bedtime beverage. So next time your mind and/or body is in desperate need of some TLC, grab a small saucepan and heat up some soothing golden milk. For a little kick, try topping your latte with freshly ground black pepper or cayenne.

1 cup coconut milk

1 teaspoon coconut oil

1 teaspoon ground turmeric (or a 1-inch piece fresh turmeric, peeled and grated)

⅛ teaspoon ground cardamom

¼ teaspoon ground cinnamon

2 teaspoons maple syrup

1 (1-inch) piece fresh ginger, peeled and roughly chopped

1 In a small saucepan, bring the coconut milk, coconut oil, turmeric, cardamom, cinnamon, maple syrup, and ginger to a boil over high heat. Reduce the heat to low and let simmer for 5 minutes.

2 Pour into a mug over a fine-mesh strainer to remove any solids.

honey cashew milk

MAKES 4 CUPS

This is my favorite nut milk, period. I put it in basically every drink to add a touch of creamy sweetness—I go through a jar every few days. It makes for a magical iced latte when mixed with two shots of espresso and poured over ice. If you prefer a nuttier taste, use half cashews and half almonds (½ cup raw almonds, ½ cup raw cashews). When the mood strikes, try adding a teaspon of your favorite warming spice, like cinnamon or cardamom, for extra flavor. Plan ahead, because the nuts require 6 to 12 hours of soaking (see Tip, page 46).

1 cup raw cashews, soaked and drained

1 to 2 tablespoons honey

1 teaspoon vanilla extract

Pinch of sea salt

1 Place the cashews, honey, vanilla, salt, and 3 cups water in a high-speed blender, and blend on high for 30 seconds, or until smooth and fully combined.

2 Using a nut-milk bag, strain the contents from your blender into a medium bowl to separate the liquid from the solids. Pour the milk into glasses to enjoy immediately or store in an airtight container in the refrigerator for up to 4 days.

matcha latte

SERVES 1

Matcha is a potent form of green tea made from ground tea leaves. For a long time, I wasn't the biggest matcha fan because it tends to be a little bitter, but blending it with Honey Cashew Milk (see page 51) perfectly tones down that earthy matcha flavor. Make your matcha bulletproof by adding ghee or coconut oil to the mix, sweeten it with a touch of honey, or blend it with a hint of rosewater. Optionally, you can sprinkle the finished latte with crushed rose petals or any other edible flowers to add a bit of extra color to your morning matcha ritual.

1 teaspoon ceremonial-grade matcha tea

½ cup hot water (not boiling)

1 cup Honey Cashew Milk, store-bought or homemade (see page 51)

In a small bowl, whisk the matcha with the hot water until fully blended. Place the matcha mixture and the milk in a high-speed blender and blend on high for 15 to 20 seconds, until fully combined. Serve over ice or enjoy warm.

cucumber watermelon rosé sangria

SERVES 4

I don't know about you, but I can't picture anything more appealing than sitting at the beach on a hot summer day with an ice-cold cocktail. Like traditional sangria, fresh fruit, wine, and liquor are mixed here and left to infuse overnight; however, this version is also filled with light, fresh, and hydrating melon and cucumber. Optionally, you can throw in some fresh mint leaves for an extra layer of refreshment.

1 bottle (750 ml) dry rosé wine

½ cup white rum

1½ cups cubed watermelon

¼ English cucumber, thinly sliced

1 cup whole mint leaves

1 cup sparkling water

1 Combine the rosé, rum, watermelon, cucumber, and mint in a large carafe or pitcher. Stir and let sit for at least 12 hours in the refrigerator before serving.

2 When you are ready to serve, add the sparkling water to the carafe. Serve chilled or over ice.

grapefruit-jalapeño margarita

SERVES *1*

The perfection of a classic margarita can't be denied, but sometimes it's fun to spice things up (literally). This grapefruit juice margarita is tart and a little sweet, with the perfect amount of heat. Salt the rim with pink Himalayan sea salt for a boost of essential minerals and a pretty pop of pink.

Ice cubes

1½ ounces (3 tablespoons) silver tequila, preferably 100% agave

Juice of ½ grapefruit (about 4 tablespoons)

Juice of 1 lime (2 tablespoons)

1 teaspoon maple syrup (optional)

1 small jalapeño pepper, sliced into thin rounds

1 to 2 teaspoons pink Himalayan sea salt, for garnish

1 lime, quartered, for garnish

1 grapefruit, halved and sliced, for garnish

1 Fill a cocktail shaker with the ice. Add the tequila, grapefruit and lime juices, maple syrup (if using), and 2 to 4 thin jalapeño slices. Shake vigorously for about 10 seconds.

2 Place the pink salt on a small plate. Use a lime wedge to wet the rim of your glass, then coat the rim with the pink salt. Fill the glass with ice cubes and pour in the drink. Garnish with a lime wedge, a half-moon grapefruit slice, and the remaining jalapeño slices.

blood orange and basil aperol spritz

SERVES 1

I just adore the bubbly, bitter taste. It's not too heavy or strong, so it's perfect for sipping on a hot afternoon. I started trying out different variations on the classic recipe and landed on this one—I never went back, and neither will you. Meet the Blood Orange and Basil Aperol Spritz. If you don't love Prosecco, you can switch the type of sparkling wine to suit your preference, but I find that the drier it is, the better.

3 ounces (6 tablespoons) Prosecco sparkling wine

2 ounces (4 tablespoons) Aperol liqueur

2 tablespoons club soda

Juice of ¼ blood orange (about 1 tablespoon)

4 to 6 fresh basil leaves

1 slice blood orange, to garnish

Fill a large white wine glass with ice, then pour in the Prosecco, Aperol, club soda, and blood orange juice. Add the basil leaves and gently stir to combine. Garnish with a blood orange slice on the rim.

passionfruit vodka martini

If you want to feel like a real mixologist, then you have to make this heavenly herbaceous and fruit-forward cocktail. The vodka is mixed with tart passionfruit pulp and sweet, floral lavender honey to ensure each sip is balanced. For a sweeter martini, use extra syrup. No matter how you shake it, this is no ordinary martini—that's for sure.

Ice cubes

1½ ounces (3 tablespoons) vodka

1 tablespoon passionfruit pulp

Juice of ½ lemon (about 1 tablespoon)

1 teaspoon Lavender Honey Syrup (recipe follows), to taste

1 sprig fresh mint, for garnish

Fill a cocktail shaker with ice cubes. Add the vodka, passionfruit, lemon juice, and Lavender Honey Syrup. Shake vigorously for 10 to 15 seconds. Pour into a martini glass and garnish with the mint sprig.

lavender honey syrup

MAKES ½ CUP

1 tablespoon dried lavender

½ cup honey

1 In a small saucepan, bring the lavender, honey, and ½ cup water to a boil over high heat. Immediately reduce the heat to medium-low and simmer, stirring occasionally, for about 3 minutes, or until the honey has fully dissolved in the water. Set aside to cool for at least 10 minutes.

2 Pour the syrup into a jar over a fine-mesh strainer to remove any solids. Use immediately or store in the refrigerator in an airtight container for up to 1 month.

breakfasts

breakfast hummus

If it were up to me, I'd eat hummus with every meal. That's precisely how this recipe was born—I wanted the option to enjoy all the flavors of a traditional bagel and lox without eating the bagel. In this breakfast remix, homemade hummus stars as the vehicle for this iconic combination. Add a poached egg if you're feeling extra hungry, and, if you're running low on time, feel free to use your favorite plain store-bought hummus.

FOR THE HUMMUS

4 garlic cloves

Juice of 1 lemon (about 2 tablespoons)

Pinch of sea salt

½ cup tahini

¼ teaspoon ground cumin

1 (15-ounce) can chickpeas, drained and rinsed

¼ cup extra-virgin olive oil

Cold water, as needed

FOR THE TOPPINGS

6 slices smoked salmon lox

1 avocado, sliced

2 Persian cucumbers, shaved into ribbons

1 tablespoon Everything Bagel Seasoning, store-bought or homemade (see page 137)

Quick Pickled Onions, to taste (see page 108)

2 poached or soft-boiled large eggs (optional; see Tips below and on page 79)

1 Make the hummus. In a food processor, combine the garlic, lemon juice, and a generous pinch of salt and pulse until the garlic is finely minced. Add in the tahini and cumin and pulse until all ingredients are fully combined.

2 To the food processor, add the chickpeas and olive oil, and puree for 1 to 2 minutes, or until smooth and creamy. Add up to 2 teaspoons of cold water as needed to thicken.

3 Divide the hummus between 2 plates, then top each with 3 slices of smoked salmon, sliced avocado, cucumber ribbons, seasoning, pickled onions, and an egg, if desired.

tip: How to poach an egg: In a medium saucepan, bring 2 cups water, 1 teaspoon apple cider vinegar, and a pinch of sea salt to a boil over high heat. Reduce the heat to medium-low and maintain a steady simmer. Crack the egg into a small dish or ramekin and then carefully add to the water, occasionally swirling and ladling the water atop the egg to help it cook. Let the egg cook for about 5 minutes, remove with a slotted spoon, and place on a paper towel–lined plate. If poaching more than one egg, add the eggs to the water one at a time.

golden yogurt bowl

SERVES *1*

If you haven't experienced the healing goodness of a Golden Milk (see page 50), then you're in for a real treat. This breakfast bowl combines inviting spices and warm flavors to create an anti-inflammatory super-meal that will keep you full for hours. For added digestive help, add a few tablespoons of fiber-rich chia seeds to make it a golden chia pudding. I like to use an unsweetened dairy-free yogurt so I have control over the amount and type of sugar I'm eating.

½ cup **nondairy yogurt** (I prefer coconut)

2 teaspoons **honey** (I like Manuka)

½ teaspoon ground **turmeric**

⅛ teaspoon ground **cardamom**

⅛ teaspoon ground **cinnamon**

1 small or ½ large **blood orange**, peel and pith removed

2 tablespoons **Toasted Pistachios** (recipe follows), crushed

1 tablespoon **unsweetened shredded coconut**

1 teaspoon **hemp seeds**

Pinch of crushed **rose petals**, for garnish

Granola Crack Clusters (see page 84; optional)

1 In a small bowl, combine the yogurt, honey, turmeric, cardamom, and cinnamon.

2 Slice the blood orange into thin rounds. To serve, top with the blood orange slices and a sprinkling of crushed pistachios, coconut, hemp seeds, rose petals, and Granola Crack Clusters (if using).

toasted pistachios
MAKES ½ CUP

½ cup shelled
pistachios

1 Finely chop the pistachios using either a knife or a food processor.

2 Heat the pistachios in a small skillet over medium heat for 5 to 10 minutes, or until the nuts start to smell fragrant and appear slightly golden in color. Use immediately or store in an airtight container at room temperature for up to 2 months.

chipotle and root vegetable scramble

SERVES 2 TO 4

I love this scramble because the entire dish can be prepped ahead of time—who has the time to peel, chop, and sauté a bunch of vegetables every morning? Eating lots of vitamin A–rich veggies can be good for balancing hormones and clearing up skin. I sauté *and* steam them so they're melt-in-your-mouth tender; and I always serve them with radish slices for a crunchy texture. I also highly recommend adding salsa, hot sauce, or sriracha for a dose of metabolism-boosting capsaicin.

1 tablespoon avocado oil

2 garlic cloves, minced

1 large red onion, sliced

½ teaspoon ground turmeric

½ teaspoon sea salt, plus more as needed

2 cups diced sweet potatoes

1 cup diced carrots

1 cup diced peeled raw beet

¼ teaspoon chipotle chile powder

¼ teaspoon onion powder

¼ teaspoon garlic powder

2 large eggs

Freshly ground black pepper

1 avocado, sliced, for garnish

1 small radish, sliced, for garnish

1 Heat ½ teaspoon of the avocado oil in a large skillet over medium heat. Once shimmering, add the garlic, red onion, turmeric, and ¼ teaspoon of the salt, and sauté for 5 minutes, or until the onion is translucent. Add the remaining 2½ teaspoons avocado oil along with the sweet potatoes, carrots, beets, remaining salt, chipotle powder, onion powder, and garlic powder. Cover and cook for 15 to 20 minutes, stirring occasionally, until fork-tender.

2 Clear a space in the center of the skillet, add the eggs, and scramble to desired doneness. Taste and season with salt and pepper. To serve, top with avocado and radish slices.

breakfast salad

SERVES 2

Anything can be a breakfast food, even salad. Salad is a crunchy green vessel for any and all the flavors and ingredients you want that also will nourish your body. In the spirit of offering a healthier alternative to the traditional American breakfast, you'll find the classic flavors here without the heavy ingredients. Think bacon, eggs, toast, and orange juice, but in leafy, green form.

6 slices pancetta (unsmoked bacon) or bacon, preferably sugar and nitrate free

1 slice gluten-free bread (or bread of your choice)

1 small butter lettuce, roughly chopped

2 cups roughly chopped radicchio

2 large eggs, fried as desired

1 avocado, sliced

1 orange, peeled and thinly sliced

2 radishes, thinly sliced

Chopped fresh mint, for garnish

1 In a large skillet, cook the pancetta over medium heat until the fat renders and the pancetta is crispy, 3 to 5 minutes per side. Drain on a paper towel–lined plate. When cool enough to handle, coarsely crumble. Reserve about 1 tablespoon of the fat in the pan.

2 In a toaster or toaster oven, toast the bread until it's golden brown, then tear into bite-sized pieces. To the same skillet, add the bread, toss with the fat until coated, and cook over medium heat for 5 to 8 minutes, or until evenly browned and crisp. Let cool on a separate paper towel–lined plate for 5 to 10 minutes.

3 Divide the lettuce and radicchio between 2 small bowls and top each with some crumbled pancetta, a fried egg, and the avocado, orange, and radish slices. Top with the croutons and sprinkle with mint.

umami granola

When you think of granola, you probably imagine sweet clusters of crunchy goodness, but savory granola opens up a whole new world of culinary possibilities. This granola is made with all the usual suspects, but uses zero sugar and gets all its flavor from spices and salty ingredients, like soy sauce, rice vinegar, and sesame oil. Use it as a crunchy topping for salads and yogurt bowls or as an alternative "breading" for fish and chicken.

½ cup cashews, roughly chopped

½ cup sliced almonds

½ cup gluten-free oats or old-fashioned rolled oats

½ cup pepitas or pumpkin seeds

½ cup hulled sunflower seeds

2 tablespoons poppy seeds

2 tablespoons sesame seeds

2 tablespoons avocado oil

1 tablespoon soy sauce or tamari

2 teaspoons toasted sesame oil

1 teaspoon rice vinegar

2 teaspoons dried minced onion

½ teaspoon garlic powder

Pinch of cayenne (optional)

Pinch of kosher salt

1 Preheat the oven to 375°F. Line a rimmed baking sheet with parchment paper.

2 In a medium bowl, combine the nuts, oats, and seeds, mixing with your hands. Add the avocado oil, soy sauce, sesame oil, rice vinegar, minced onion, garlic powder, cayenne (if using), and salt, and toss well with a spoon to combine.

3 Spread the granola in an even layer on the baking sheet. Bake, stirring halfway through, until fragrant and golden brown, 10 to 12 minutes. Let the granola sit for 20 minutes to fully cool and harden.

4 Break the granola into clusters. Store in an airtight jar at room temperature for 3 to 4 weeks.

persian breakfast platter

SERVES *2* TO *4*

My Iranian American fiancé, Arash, introduced me to traditional Persian breakfasts. The table is adorned with a smorgasbord of spreads and toppings, which typically includes sabzi (fresh herbs), radishes, cucumbers, walnuts, honey, soft cheese, and jam, along with a delicious flatbread called "lavash," "barbari," or "sangak." To make it a little more gut-friendly, I created this grain-free homage to this delicious breakfast spread. The best part of a Persian breakfast is that you can make all kinds of delicious combinations; my favorite is goat or sheep's milk feta, honey, fresh mint, walnuts, and fresh figs.

FOR THE FLATBREADS

¼ cup almond flour

¼ cup chickpea flour

½ cup tapioca flour

¼ teaspoon sea salt

½ tablespoon sesame seeds

1 cup canned coconut milk

FOR THE TOPPINGS

Handful of fresh basil leaves

Handful of fresh parsley leaves

Handful of fresh mint leaves

4 small radishes, halved

4 Persian cucumbers, sliced

½ cup whole walnuts

2 tablespoons honey

¼ cup crumbled feta cheese

5 to 10 fresh figs (optional)

1 Make the flatbreads. In a medium bowl, combine the flours, salt, sesame seeds, and coconut milk and stir with a spoon until most of the lumps have disappeared.

2 Preheat a large nonstick skillet over high heat for 2 to 3 minutes. Pour ¼ cup of the batter into the skillet, and spread it out until it is as thin as possible. Cook for about 5 minutes, or until you see bubbles start to form, then flip and cook 5 minutes more, or until crisp with golden brown spots. Remove the flatbread and set aside while you make the remaining breads. This batter should make 6 large flatbreads.

3 Arrange all the herbs, radishes, cucumbers, walnuts, honey, feta cheese, and figs (if using) on a platter alongside the flatbreads.

savory oatmeal

SERVES *2*

This savory oatmeal is the ultimate comfort food; it's the delicious intersection of traditional oatmeal, risotto, and congee. I always thought of oatmeal as a sweet breakfast food, so when I discovered the simplicity of oats drizzled with olive oil and sea salt, it was life changing. I couldn't stop eating it, and neither will you! Adding a runny soft-boiled egg, creamy avocado, and caramelized onions is my favorite iteration. Plus, it's the perfect meal to make ahead of time: simply cook the oats the night before, then heat it up and add the toppings in the morning.

2 cups water

Sea salt

1 cup gluten-free oats (or oats of your choice)

2 tablespoons avocado oil

1 medium onion, halved and sliced

½ teaspoon sweet paprika

2 large soft-boiled eggs (see Tip)

1 avocado, sliced

¼ cup watermelon radish, minced (about ½ radish)

2 teaspoons Everything Bagel Seasoning, store-bought or homemade (see page 137)

Crushed red pepper flakes, to taste

1 In a medium saucepan, bring 2 cups water and a pinch of salt to a boil over high heat. Add the oats and give them a quick stir. Reduce the heat to medium-low and cook for 15 minutes, or until all the water has been absorbed and the oats are fluffy.

2 In a medium skillet, heat the avocado oil over medium-high heat. When the oil shimmers, add the onion, paprika, and ¼ teaspoon salt, and cook until the onion is caramelized, about 10 minutes.

3 Divide the oats between 2 bowls. Top each with some caramelized onion, a soft-boiled egg, the avocado, watermelon radish, seasoning, and crushed red pepper flakes, and serve.

tip: How to soft-boil an egg: Bring 2 cups of water to a rapid boil in a medium pot over high heat. While the water is coming to a boil, prepare a small bowl filled with ice water and set aside. Add the egg(s) and boil for exactly 6 minutes, then, using tongs or a slatted spoon, transfer the eggs to the bowl of ice water to stop the cooking.

pink chia pudding
with cinnamon broiled peach

SERVES *1* TO *2*

The star of this recipe is the cinnamon broiled peach. Every time I smell or taste a baked, roasted, broiled, or stewed peach, I immediately think of peach cobbler, and, in my humble opinion, there's really nothing better than dessert for breakfast. Feel free to add as many or as few extra toppings as you'd like. In case you were wondering, some of my favorites are peeled and sliced orange, granola, edible flowers, dried mulberries or goji berries, and fresh mint leaves.

1 cup Pink Rosewater Cashew Milk (see page 46)

3 tablespoons chia seeds

1 ripe peach, sliced

½ teaspoon coconut oil (melted or solid is fine)

Pinch of ground cinnamon

Pinch of kosher salt

1 tablespoon Toasted Pistachios, store-bought or homemade (see page 67)

1 Preheat the broiler. Line a baking sheet with parchment paper.

2 In a small bowl, combine the cashew milk and chia seeds and let sit for 10 minutes, until the chia seeds are gelatinous and the combined mixture is thick enough to resemble a pudding.

3 In a separate small bowl, combine the peach slices, coconut oil, cinnamon, and salt, and toss until coated. Evenly space the peaches on the baking sheet and broil for 10 minutes.

4 Top the chia pudding with the broiled peaches and pistachios to serve.

chili-passionfruit salad

SERVES 1 TO 2

Fruit salad is a beloved classic, but it's even better with a spicy kick. There's just something about the juxtaposition of spicy and sweet that makes my taste buds happy—not to mention that the capsaicin in the chili revs up your metabolism. In Miami, most tropical fruits are available year-round, but if any of the fruits are not in season or available near you, simply substitute your favorite seasonal fruits.

1 mandarin, peeled and sliced

1 blood orange, peeled and sliced

1 cup diced papaya (about ½ Caribbean papaya)

1 dragon fruit, diced

1 ripe peach or nectarine, sliced

2 fresh passionfruits, halved and scooped out (see Tip)

¼ cup thinly sliced fresh mint leaves

½ teaspoon Aleppo pepper

Juice of ½ orange (about 1 tablespoon)

1 In a medium bowl, combine the mandarin, blood orange, papaya, dragon fruit, peach, passionfruit pulp, mint leaves, Aleppo pepper, and orange juice. Let the fruit marinate in the fridge for at least 10 minutes to allow the flavors to blend.

2 Store in an airtight container in the refrigerator for up to 3 days. Best served chilled.

tip: To access the passionfruit pulp, simply cut the passionfruit in half and scoop out the yellow/orange flesh, seeds, and juice. If you don't have any Aleppo pepper on hand, substitute with crushed red pepper flakes.

granola crack clusters

At the intersection of sticky and crunchy, you will find these highly addictive granola crack clusters. Some of this entirely grain-free granola will crumble (as expected), but it's those small clusters that get stuck together in the baking process that you won't be able to stop eating. You can top them with milk and eat them like cereal, mix them into your favorite yogurt, or use them as a garnish on a smoothie bowl. They also make for a delicious snack on their own.

2 cups sliced almonds

1 cup crushed walnut pieces

½ cup raw pumpkin seeds

¼ cup chia seeds

¼ cup sunflower seeds

¼ cup coconut oil

½ cup plus 1 tablespoon maple syrup

¼ teaspoon sea salt

1 Preheat the oven to 350°F. Line a rimmed baking sheet with parchment paper.

2 In a large bowl, combine the almonds, walnuts, pumpkin seeds, chia seeds, and sunflower seeds until evenly mixed.

3 Heat the coconut oil and maple syrup in a medium saucepan over low heat until the oil is melted, then stir to combine. Pour the mixture evenly over the nut mixture and toss well to evenly coat. Spread the granola in an even layer on the baking sheet.

4 Bake for 15 to 20 minutes, or until golden brown and sticky. Let the granola cool until it is room temperature, then break it up. Store in an airtight container at room temperature for up to 2 months.

tahdig
eggs benedict

It's hard to believe there was a time in my life when I was not eating tahdig—aka Persian crispy rice (introducing me to it is high up there on the list of reasons I love Arash). It literally means "bottom of the pot" because it's the crispy saffron rice scraped from, you guessed it, the bottom of the pot. The traditional cooking method is more of an art and rather extensive, involving soaking, par cooking, and carefully placed holes for steam. So for the sake of ease, I usually go with my lazy rice cooker version.

FOR THE TAHDIG

½ cup white basmati rice

1½ tablespoons unsalted butter

Pinch of sea salt

FOR THE SAFFRON

½ teaspoon ground saffron

2 tablespoons hot water, not quite boiling

FOR THE CASHEW HOLLANDAISE

½ cup cashews, soaked for at least 2 hours and drained

2 tablespoons extra-virgin olive oil

½ teaspoon rosewater

1 garlic clove

½ teaspoon honey

¼ teaspoon sea salt

2 large poached eggs (see Tip, page 64)

½ teaspoon ground sumac, for garnish

1 tablespoon fresh parsley, finely chopped, for garnish

1 Make the tahdig. To a rice cooker, add the rice, ¾ cup water, the butter, and a pinch of sea salt, stir to combine, and set to "cook."

2 Meanwhile, make the saffron. In a small bowl, combine the saffron and hot water, stir, and cover with foil or a dish towel and set aside.

3 Once the rice is done, wait a few minutes and set to "cook" again. Repeat the cook cycle 3 more times (about 45 minutes total) to ensure that the rice is crisping. Drizzle ½ teaspoon of the saffron evenly over the rice and "cook" the rice one more time.

4 Meanwhile, make the hollandaise. In a food processor, combine the cashews, olive oil, remaining saffron liquid, rosewater, garlic, honey, salt, and ½ cup water and puree until the hollandaise thickens slightly but is still easy to pour.

5 Using oven mitts, remove the pot from the rice cooker, then cover with a large plate, and invert it, releasing all the loose rice and the crispy crust onto the plate.

6 To assemble, divide the loose rice between two bowls. Top each with a large piece of the tahdig, a poached egg, hollandaise, sumac, and parsley.

bowls

banh mi hummus and lemongrass chicken

SERVES *2* TO *4*

I love hummus because it's so versatile; you can top it with just about anything and it will taste amazing. That's why I've put all the fixings of a Vietnamese banh mi sandwich in a hummus bowl: the umami flavor of the hummus perfectly complements the fresh herbs and pickled vegetables. For the hummus, I've used red lentils instead of garbanzo beans because they have a super creamy, velvety texture that goes perfectly with the crunchy, vinegary quick-pickled veggies.

FOR THE CHICKEN

4 garlic cloves, minced

1 shallot, minced

1 lemongrass stalk, minced (about 2 tablespoons)

1 teaspoon rice vinegar

4 tablespoons fish sauce

¼ teaspoon crushed red pepper flakes

2 teaspoons coconut sugar

3 tablespoons avocado oil

Juice of ½ lime (about 1 tablespoon)

4 (4-ounce) boneless, skinless chicken breasts or tenders

FOR THE HUMMUS

1 cup red lentils

4 garlic cloves

1 small shallot

2 tablespoons fish sauce

Juice of 1 lime (about 2 tablespoons)

2 tablespoons avocado oil

2 teaspoons coconut sugar

¼ teaspoon crushed red pepper flakes

2 teaspoons tamarind paste or rice vinegar

FOR THE QUICK-PICKLED BANH MI VEGETABLES

1 cup shredded carrot

1 cup thinly sliced daikon radish

1 cup julienned Persian cucumber

3 tablespoons rice vinegar

1 tablespoon coconut sugar

½ teaspoon sea salt

½ cup chopped fresh mint leaves, for garnish

½ cup chopped fresh cilantro leaves, for garnish

1 Make the chicken. In a food processor, puree the garlic, shallot, lemongrass, vinegar, fish sauce, red pepper flakes, coconut sugar, 2 tablespoons of the avocado oil, and lime juice until garlic, shallot, and lemongrass are finely minced and a sauce is formed. Place the chicken in a large bowl and pour the marinade over until the chicken is completely submerged. Cover with plastic and let marinate in the refrigerator for 6 hours to overnight.

2 Make the hummus. In a medium saucepan, bring the lentils and 4 cups water to a boil over high heat, then reduce the heat to medium-low and simmer, half-covered, for 25 to 30 minutes, or until soft and mushy. Drain any excess liquid and let cool for at least 10 minutes.

3 Meanwhile, make the quick-pickled vegetables. In a medium bowl, combine the carrot, radish, cucumber, rice vinegar, coconut sugar, and salt. Let the vegetables sit in the brine, uncovered, at room temperature for at least 30 minutes.

4 In a food processor, pulse the garlic and shallot until very finely minced. Then, add the cooked lentils, fish sauce, lime juice, avocado oil, coconut sugar, red pepper flakes, and tamarind. Puree until smooth and creamy, about 5 minutes. Taste and adjust as needed. Add more vinegar or tamarind for acid, and fish sauce for salt.

5 In a large skillet, heat the remaining tablespoon avocado oil over medium-high heat. Once shimmering, add the marinated chicken. Cook undisturbed for 5 to 7 minutes, then flip and cook 10 minutes more, until the chicken is cooked through and browned on all sides. Let the chicken rest for at least 5 minutes before slicing.

6 To assemble, spoon 1 cup of hummus into a shallow bowl or onto a plate and top with some chicken and pickled vegetables, then garnish with mint and cilantro to taste. Store leftovers separately in airtight containers in the refrigerator for up to a week.

chipotle lentil taco salad

SERVES *2*

Is there anything the almighty lentil can't do? This is a question I ask myself often. Lentils are my favorite because they are insanely easy to make and have a shocking amount of protein (18 grams per cup!). They also have such a hearty and grounding quality, making them the perfect plant-based protein alternative to many meals that typically use meat. You can use lentils to make pasta, burgers, meatballs—you name it! And, in this recipe, we're using them in place of taco meat. You'll be getting all the taco flavor, but with way more gut healthy fiber—win win!

FOR THE LENTILS

2 tablespoons avocado oil

1 red onion, sliced

1 bell pepper, thinly sliced

½ teaspoon chipotle powder

1 teaspoon garlic powder

Kosher salt

1 cup black lentils, cooked and drained

¼ teaspoon ground cumin

FOR THE PICO DE GALLO

2 cups cherry tomatoes, diced

½ cup cilantro, chopped

2 garlic cloves, minced

½ white onion, diced

½ jalapeno, diced

Juice of ½ a lime (1 tablespoon lime juice)

FOR THE SALAD

1 avocado, mashed

2 heads of romaine, shredded

½ cup frozen corn, thawed and drained

2 to 3 tablespoons Spicy Lime Chipotle Dressing (recipe follows)

1 Make the lentils. In a large skillet, heat the avocado oil over medium heat. When the oil is shimmering, add the red onion, bell pepper, chipotle powder, garlic powder, and a pinch of salt. Cook for 5 to 10 minutes, until the onions and peppers have softened. Add in the cooked lentils, cumin, and another pinch of salt. Reduce the heat to low, stir to combine, and cook 5 minutes more, or until the flavors meld together.

2 Meanwhile, make the pico de gallo. In a small bowl, combine the cherry tomatoes, cilantro, garlic, white onion, jalapeño, lime juice, and salt, and toss to coat.

3 Make the salad. In a large bowl, combine the avocado, romaine, and corn and toss. Drizzle with the Spicy Lime Chipotle Dressing and toss to coat. Divide the salad between two bowls and top each with a big spoonful of the lentil mixture and the pico de gallo. Serve immediately.

spicy chipotle lime dressing
MAKES ¼ CUP

2 garlic cloves, minced

Juice of ½ lime (1 tablespoon lime juice)

¼ teaspoon cumin

1 tablespoon avocado oil

2 tablespoons veganaise or mayonnaise

¼ teaspoon crushed red pepper flakes

⅛ teaspoon ground chipotle pepper

½ teaspoon honey

In a small bowl, combine the garlic, lime juice, cumin, avocado oil, veganaise, crushed red pepper flakes, chipotle pepper, and honey and whisk until fully combined. Store the dressing in an airtight container in the fridge for up to 1 week.

tahini honey-mustard kale salad

SERVES *2*

When you hear "kale salad," you probably don't start salivating—I, too, have had one too many rough and flavorless kale salads that feel like munching on a bowl of twigs and leaves. The key to achieving an amazing kale salad, besides using a killer dressing, is to massage the kale. Yes, you read that right. Toss the kale in some fat, acid, and salt to break down that roughness and get your hands in that salad bowl. I prefer curly kale for my salads because I find it to be softer and more palatable.

1 Tear the kale into bite-sized pieces, then add to a large bowl along with the olive oil, vinegar, and salt and massage for 30 seconds or until the kale appears softened and deeper in color. Add the chickpeas, radish, cucumbers, hemp seeds, and nutritional yeast.

2 Drizzle the Tahini Mustard Honey, and toss to combine. Serve immediately.

tahini honey mustard
MAKES *¼* CUP

1 bunch curly kale, washed and stemmed

1 teaspoon extra-virgin olive oil

½ teaspoon apple cider vinegar

½ teaspoon salt

½ cup Crunchy Chickpeas (see page 117)

1 watermelon radish, diced (optional)

2 Persian cucumbers, sliced (optional)

1 tablespoon hemp seeds

1 tablespoon nutritional yeast

2 to 3 tablespoons Tahini Honey Mustard (recipe follows)

1 tablespoon tahini

Juice of 1 lemon (2 tablespoons)

2 teaspoons extra-virgin olive oil

¼ teaspoon salt

1 teaspoon Dijon mustard

1 teaspoon honey

Water, as needed

1 In a small bowl, combine the tahini, lemon juice, olive oil, salt, mustard, and honey. Whisk the dressing until fully emulsified and combined. Whisk in up to 2 teaspoons water to thin as needed.

2 Store the dressing in a small airtight jar in the refrigerator for up to 1 week.

peachy arugula salad

SERVES *2*

Stone fruit season is my absolute favorite. In the summer, I rarely eat a salad without adding peaches, plums, or apricots. Arugula is bursting with nutrients and its bold, nutty flavor goes perfectly with sweet toppings. This juicy, tart salad is a great first course for your next summertime soiree, but don't make this salad when peaches are out of season—it won't taste nearly as delicious if you use canned—plus, it's good to support local farmers.

3 cups fresh arugula

½ radicchio, roughly chopped

¼ cup fresh basil leaves, thinly sliced

¼ cup fresh mint leaves, thinly sliced

2 Persian cucumbers, shaved into ribbons

1 small watermelon radish, sliced

1 fresh peach, sliced

¼ cup Toasted Pistachios (see page 67), finely chopped

¼ cup hulled sunflower seeds

2 to 3 tablespoons Lemony Balsamic Dressing (recipe follows)

In a large bowl, combine the arugula, radicchio, basil, mint, cucumber, watermelon radish, peach, pistachios, and sunflower seeds. Drizzle the Lemony Balsamic Dressing over the salad and toss until well coated. Divide the salad between 2 bowls and serve immediately.

lemony balsamic dressing

MAKES ¼ CUP

2 tablespoons extra-virgin olive oil

1 tablespoon balsamic vinegar

1 teaspoon Dijon mustard

½ teaspoon raw honey

Juice of ½ lemon (1 tablespoon)

½ teaspoon grated lemon zest (optional)

Kosher salt and freshly ground black pepper, to taste

1 In a small bowl, combine the olive oil, vinegar, mustard, honey, lemon juice, and zest, and whisk until smooth.

2 Store the dressing in a small airtight jar in the refrigerator for up to 1 week.

pink caesar salad

SERVES 2

I've been making this dairy-free Caesar for years, and it always hits the spot. True to form, I decided to try making it pink with beet juice—beautiful color and some earthy flavor, what's not to love? The dressing gets its cheesy flavor from the nutritional yeast and its anchovy taste from a few dashes of fish sauce. I also like to break up some Almond Chia Crackers to use as a crouton substitute, but feel free to omit if you don't have any. Also, feel free to use any other type of lettuce in this salad, and add crunchy vegetables (like chopped cucumbers and carrots) or top with some seared chicken or salmon.

2 heads of romaine lettuce, torn into bite-sized pieces

2 tablespoons hemp seeds

2 tablespoons nutritional yeast

2 to 3 tablespoons Pink Caesar Dressing (recipe follows)

10 Almond Chia Crackers (see page 188), crumbled (optional)

Place the romaine in a large salad bowl and toss with the hemp seeds, nutritional yeast, and Creamy Pink Caesar Dressing. Divide the salad between 2 bowls and top with the crumbled crackers, if desired. Serve immediately.

creamy pink caesar dressing
MAKES 1 CUP

4 garlic cloves

½ shallot

⅓ cup veganaise or mayonnaise

1 tablespoon extra-virgin olive oil

3 tablespoons nutritional yeast

2 tablespoons beet juice (or 1 tablespoon chopped peeled raw beet)

1 teaspoon fish sauce or caper juice

1 teaspoon Dijon mustard

1 teaspoon apple cider vinegar

½ teaspoon freshly ground black pepper

1 To a food processor or high-speed blender, add the garlic and shallot and pulse until finely minced. Add in the veganaise, olive oil, nutritional yeast, beet juice, fish sauce, mustard, apple cider vinegar, and black pepper, and puree until smooth.

2 The dressing is best if used right away, but can be stored in an airtight container in the refrigerator for up to 2 days.

toasted pepita plum salad

SERVES *1* TO *2*

Whether you call them pumpkin seeds or pepitas, these impressive little seeds boast quite a résumé. They are loaded with protein (12 grams per cup!), magnesium, and potassium, not to mention they are a great source of dietary fiber (12 grams per cup). They also have a high level of zinc, which is great for treating acne. Pumpkin seeds can be eaten roasted or raw, hulled or in a shell, salted or unsalted, but toasting them brings out a delicious nutty flavor and adds a nice crunch to anything you put them on.

1 tablespoon pepitas

1 cup torn butter lettuce, in bite-sized pieces

1 cup torn radicchio, in bite-sized pieces

½ avocado, cubed

1 small golden beet, peeled and thinly sliced

1 small watermelon radish, halved and thinly sliced

1 teaspoon hemp seeds

1 fresh plum, sliced

2 tablespoons crumbed goat cheese

2 to 3 tablespoons "Put This on Everything" Dressing (recipe follows)

1 In a small dry skillet, toast the pepitas over medium-high heat for 2 to 3 minutes, or until fragrant.

2 Place the toasted pepitas in a large bowl, and add the lettuce, radicchio, avocado, beet, watermelon radish, hemp seeds, plum, and goat cheese. Stir and then drizzle with the "Put This on Everything" dressing. Toss until evenly coated. Divide the salad between 2 bowls and serve immediately.

"put this on everything" dressing MAKES ¼ CUP

3 garlic cloves, minced

1 teaspoon Dijon mustard

2 tablespoons extra-virgin olive oil

1 tablespoon apple cider vinegar

¼ teaspoon sea salt

½ shallot, minced (optional)

2 tablespoons chopped fresh parsley (optional)

In a small bowl, combine the garlic, mustard, olive oil, vinegar, salt, shallot, and parsley, and whisk vigorously until emulsified. Store the dressing in an airtight container in the refrigerator for up to 1 week.

watermelon sumac salad

SERVES 2

Watermelon is perfect all on its own, but in the warm summer months, I add this hydrating melon to as many meals as possible. A feta and watermelon salad is classic, and for good reason: the salty cheese combined with the sweet, refreshing melon is a match made in salad heaven. I throw in some fresh mint and Middle Eastern spices like sumac and za'atar for a kick of flavor.

4 cups cubed seedless **watermelon**

⅓ cup **Quick Pickled Onions** (recipe follows)

⅓ cup crumbled **feta cheese**

⅓ cup thinly sliced fresh **mint leaves**

2 tablespoons crushed **Toasted Pistachios** (see page 67)

1 tablespoon **extra-virgin olive oil**

½ teaspoon ground **sumac**

½ teaspoon **za'atar**

In a large bowl, combine the watermelon, pickled onions, feta, mint, pistachios, olive oil, sumac, and za'atar. Toss until evenly distributed. Divide between 2 bowls and serve immediately.

quick pickled onions

MAKES 2 CUPS (16 OUNCES)

½ cup **rice vinegar**

2 tablespoons **honey** or **coconut sugar**

1 teaspoon **sea salt**

1 **red onion**, thinly sliced

1 small or ½ large **jalapeño pepper**, with seeds (optional)

¼ cup chopped peeled fresh **beet** (optional)

1 In a medium saucepan, bring 1 cup water, vinegar, honey, and salt to a boil over high heat. Reduce the heat to medium-low and simmer for at least 5 minutes, or until the honey is dissolved.

2 Place the red onion, jalapeño, and beet in a 16-ounce glass jar, then pour in the pickling liquid and cover with an airtight lid. Let cool completely, then chill in the refrigerator for at least 2 hours. Store in an airtight jar in the refrigerator for up to 1 month.

glow bowl

SERVES _1_

Spoiler alert: I am obsessed with lentils. They're so easy to cook, extremely versatile, and a high-quality source of plant-based protein. Beyond the healthy protein, this bowl is bursting with glow-inducing fats from the omega-3s in the salmon and avocado. Also, the microgreens pack a macro-nutrient punch, so sprinkle them around your plate like confetti. When your skin needs some love, whip up this bowl and reap the benefits.

1 cup **black lentils** (I like beluga)

1 (2- to 3-ounce) **salmon fillet**

½ **shallot**, minced

Juice of ½ **lemon** (about 1 tablespoon)

¼ teaspoon **sweet paprika**

1 **garlic clove**, minced

2 pinches of **salt**

1 **orange slice** (optional)

1 tablespoon **Green Sauce** (see page 167)

1 tablespoon **veganaise** or **mayonnaise**

1 tablespoon **olive oil**

¼ cup **microgreens** or **sprouts**, for serving

1 **radish** or **beet**, sliced, for garnish

½ **avocado**, sliced, for garnish

_1_ Preheat the broiler.

_2_ In medium saucepan, bring 4 cups water to a boil over high heat. Add the lentils and reduce the heat to medium-low. Simmer, half-covered, for 20 to 25 minutes, or until the lentils are fork-tender. Drain the lentils and set aside to cool for 10 minutes.

_3_ Meanwhile, place the salmon skin side down on a baking sheet and top with the shallot, lemon juice, paprika, garlic, a pinch of salt, and the orange slice (if using). Broil for 8 minutes, or until salmon appears opaque throughout.

_4_ In a small bowl or ramekin, whisk the green sauce and veganaise until smooth.

_5_ Drain the lentils and mix them with the olive oil and remaining salt. To assemble, top the lentils with the salmon, garnish with the microgreens, radish, and avocado, and drizzle with the green mayonnaise.

fish taco bowls

SERVES *2* TO *4*

When I was growing up, one of my favorite nights of the week was when we'd have fish tacos. We would typically use beer-battered fried cod, which is super tasty but not exactly healthy. For this lighter twist on fish tacos, I opted for a bed of lettuce instead of a heavier tortilla. This is a healthy, easy recipe to make for your next gathering. You can even set out all the ingredients and have your friends build their own "taco bowls."

FOR THE FISH

2 garlic cloves, minced

Juice of ½ lime (1 tablespoon)

1 tablespoon avocado oil

¼ teaspoon salt

¼ teaspoon chipotle chile powder

4 (6-ounce) cod fillets

FOR THE PICO DE GALLO

1 cup diced mango (from 1 ripe mango)

½ cup diced onion

1 jalapeño pepper, minced

¼ cup fresh cilantro leaves, finely chopped

Juice of 1 lime (2 tablespoons)

¼ teaspoon sea salt

FOR THE MAYO

3 tablespoons mayonnaise or veganaise

1 tablespoon sriracha

Juice of ½ lime (1 tablespoon)

½ teaspoon honey

¼ teaspoon ground cumin

FOR THE SALAD

2 cups shredded iceberg lettuce

2 cups shredded romaine

1 cup thinly sliced green cabbage

TOPPINGS (OPTIONAL)

1 cup crushed tortilla chips

2 watermelon radishes, thinly sliced

1 avocado, sliced

⅓ cup chopped fresh cilantro

1 Preheat the broiler and line a baking sheet with parchment paper.

2 Make the fish. In a small bowl, combine the garlic, lime juice, avocado oil, salt, and chipotle powder. Add the fish and evenly coat with the garlic mixture. Place the fish on the baking sheet and broil for 10 minutes, until opaque and flakey. Let the fish cool for 5 to 10 minutes, then break up into bite-sized pieces using a fork.

3 Meanwhile, make the pico de gallo. In a small bowl, combine the mango, onion, jalapeño, cilantro, lime juice, and salt.

4 Make the mayo. In a small bowl, whisk together the mayonnaise, sriracha, lime juice, honey, and cumin until a smooth, creamy sauce forms.

5 Divide the lettuce and cabbage among 4 bowls and top each with some chunks of cod. Drizzle with the mayo and top with the pico de gallo. Sprinkle on the tortilla chips, radishes, avocado, and cilantro, if desired.

coconut quinoa bowl

SERVES *1* **TO** *2*

Creamy coconut rice is so comforting and delicious that I took those flavors and made them with quinoa, which is one of the most nutrient-dense grains around. It's loaded with protein and has a lot more fiber than rice. Cooking the quinoa in a mixture of half water and half coconut milk also makes it oh so fluffy and it feels even heartier. The best part? Coconut quinoa tastes even better the next day. P.S. When using coconut milk for cooking, opt for full fat culinary grade typically found in a can in the international section of your grocery store!

½ cup **quinoa**, rinsed and drained

1 (15-ounce) can **full-fat coconut milk**

¼ teaspoon **sea salt**

¼ cup diced **radish**

¼ cup diced **cucumber**

2 tablespoons **Crunchy Chickpeas** (recipe follows)

1 to 2 tablespoons **pomegranate seeds**

2 tablespoons crumbled **feta cheese**

Small handful of fresh **mint leaves**

Small handful of fresh **basil leaves**

Small handful of **sprouts** or **microgreens**

1 In a medium saucepan, bring the quinoa, coconut milk, ⅓ cup water, and salt to a boil over high heat. Reduce the heat to medium-low, cover, and simmer for 20 to 25 minutes, or until the liquid is fully absorbed and the quinoa is fluffy.

2 Place the quinoa in each bowl and top with the radish, cucumber, chickpeas, pomegranate seeds, and feta, then sprinkle with the mint, basil, and sprouts.

crunchy chickpeas

MAKES ABOUT *2* CUPS

1 (15-ounce) can
chickpeas

½ teaspoon
sweet paprika

1 teaspoon
avocado oil

½ teaspoon
garlic powder

¼ teaspoon
sea salt

¼ teaspoon
cayenne

1 Preheat the oven to 400°F and line a baking sheet with parchment paper.

2 Strain and rinse the chickpeas, then pat dry. On the baking sheet, toss the chickpeas with the avocado oil, salt, paprika, garlic powder, and cayenne. Roast the chickpeas for 20 minutes, or until golden brown and crispy. Store in an airtight jar at room temperature for up to 2 weeks.

shrimp and hearts of palm chopped salad

SERVES *2* TO *4*

I live for a chopped salad. All the ingredients are perfectly distributed into bite-sized forkfuls. There's no awkwardly cramming too-big pieces of lettuce into your mouth! The added bonus of this particular chopped salad is that it's hearty and filling. I love it so much that sometimes, when I make this for dinner, I make a huge portion (hold the dressing) and store the remainder in the fridge so I can pack it in my lunch for days. Meal-prep alert!

1 tablespoon unsalted butter

2 garlic cloves, minced

1 pound medium shrimp

Juice of ½ lemon (1 tablespoon)

½ teaspoon sea salt

2 teaspoons avocado oil

2 large shallots, thinly sliced

½ iceberg lettuce, finely chopped

1 romaine lettuce, finely chopped

2 cups finely chopped fresh arugula

⅓ cup finely chopped fresh parsley

½ English cucumber or 2 Persian cucumbers, diced (about 1 cup)

4 small radishes, diced

1 avocado, diced

1 (15-ounce) can hearts of palm, diced

2 to 3 tablespoons Creamy Garlic Dijon Dressing (recipe follows)

1 In a large skillet, combine the butter and garlic over medium heat. When the butter is melted, add the shrimp, lemon juice, and salt, and cook, stirring occasionally, for 6 minutes, or until the shrimp is opaque and pink. Let cool completely, about 10 minutes.

2 Wipe out the skillet, then heat the avocado oil over medium-high heat. When the oil is shimmering, add the shallots and cook, stirring frequently, for 5 to 7 minutes, or until crispy and evenly browned. Place on a paper towel–lined plate to drain.

3 In a large bowl, combine the lettuce, arugula, parsley, cucumber, radish, avocado, and hearts of palm. Finely chop the shrimp and add it to the salad along with the fried shallots.

4 Drizzle the salad with the Creamy Garlic Dijon Dressing and toss until evenly coated. Divide among bowls to serve immediately.

creamy garlic dijon dressing
MAKES ¼ CUP

3 garlic cloves, minced

1½ tablespoons Dijon mustard

2 tablespoons veganaise or mayonnaise

3 tablespoons extra-virgin olive oil

1 tablespoon apple cider vinegar

Juice of ½ lemon (1 tablespoon)

Kosher salt and freshly ground black pepper, to taste

In a small bowl, combine the garlic, mustard, veganaise, olive oil, apple cider vinegar, lemon juice, salt, and pepper to taste, and whisk until fully combined. Store the dressing in a small airtight jar in the refrigerator for up to 1 week.

toasts

sweet potatoast, three ways

SERVES 2

When you're craving the simplicity and comfort of a piece of toast but you're taking a break from bread, sweet potato toast comes in mighty handy. Beyond the idea itself, what I love about sweet potato toast is its endless versatility. You can top a sweet potato slice with *anything* your heart desires. Enter these three delicious toasts.

1 large **sweet potato (skin on)**, cut crosswise into 4 slices 1½ inches thick

½ teaspoon **avocado** or **coconut oil**

Pinch of **sea salt**

1 Preheat the oven to 400°F and line a rimmed baking sheet with parchment paper.

2 Place the sweet potato slices on the baking sheet and toss with the avocado oil and salt. Roast for 15 minutes, then flip over the slices and cook for 15 minutes more, or until lightly browned and fork-tender. Let cool for 10 minutes, then top with your preferred variation.

everything avocado variation SERVES 2

1 teaspoon
Everything Bagel
Seasoning (see
page 137)

1 avocado,
sliced

½ radish,
diced

Top each slice of toasted sweet
potato with Everything Bagel
Seasoning, avocado, and diced radish.

cinnamon almond-butter banana variation SERVES 2

2 teaspoons
almond butter
(or nut butter of
your choice)

½ a banana, sliced
into rounds

Pinch of sea salt

Pinch of ground
cinnamon

1 teaspoon
Pistachio Coconut
Rose Dukkah
(optional; see
page 33)

Top each slice of toasted sweet potato
with 2 teaspoons almond butter, slices
of ½ banana, a small pinch of sea salt
and ground cinnamon, and, if desired,
1 teaspoon of Pistachio Coconut Rose
Dukkah.

stone fruit and basil variation SERVES 2

2 teaspoons cream
cheese (nondairy
or regular)

½ a plum (or
stone fruit of your
choice)

4 leaves of
fresh basil

Top each slice of toasted sweet potato
with 2 teaspoons cream cheese, slices of
½ plum, and a few leaves of fresh basil.

loaded avocado toast

SERVES *2*

If being a typical avocado toast–obsessed millennial is wrong, then I don't want to be right. Avocado toast is the best— plain and simple. It's probably the most photographed toast in the game, it's indisputably tasty, and it's really easy to make. But there's nothing plain about this loaded variation. I love taking the visual aspects of avocado toast up a notch by adding vibrant colors like orange from freshly grated turmeric and hot pink from sliced watermelon radish.

1 In a toaster or toaster oven, toast the bread to your preference.

2 In a small bowl, mash the avocado using a fork until it is easily spreadable, then add the garlic and combine. Spread the avocado-garlic mixture evenly on each slice of toast.

3 Top with the peas, mint, radish, turmeric, and hemp seeds, then drizzle with the olive oil and lemon juice and season to taste with salt and pepper.

2 slices bread of your choice

1 avocado

2 garlic cloves, minced

4 sugar-snap peas, trimmed and chopped

6 fresh mint leaves, thinly sliced

2 watermelon radish slices, cut into matchsticks

1 (½-inch) piece fresh turmeric root, grated

½ teaspoon hemp seeds

½ teaspoon extra-virgin olive oil

½ teaspoon lemon juice

Kosher salt and freshly ground black pepper, to taste

caramelized
banana toast

I would categorize this recipe as a dessert toast, as it will satisfy a sweet tooth of any size using only the natural sugars of a banana and a touch of pure maple syrup. Topping the toast with lemon zest adds brightness, while the cinnamon adds a warm, cozy flavor. Imagine curling up on a rainy Sunday with this caramelized banana toast in hand—I've been there, and I can tell you there is nothing more comforting.

1 slice bread of your choice

1 teaspoon coconut oil

1 teaspoon maple syrup

1 banana, thickly sliced

2 tablespoons thick yogurt (I like coconut flavor)

1 teaspoon sliced almonds (or other nuts of your choice)

¼ teaspoon grated lemon zest

1 teaspoon hemp seeds

Pinch of ground cinnamon

Pinch of sea salt

1 teaspoon honey, optional

1 In a toaster or toaster oven, toast the bread to your preference.

2 In a small pan, heat the coconut oil and maple syrup over medium-high heat until the coconut oil is melted. Add the banana slices and cook for 5 minutes, flipping halfway through, or until golden brown and caramelized on both sides.

3 Spread the yogurt thickly on the toast and top with the caramelized banana, almonds, lemon zest, hemp seeds, cinnamon, salt, and a drizzle of honey.

chocolate tahini passionfruit toast

SERVES 1

It's hard to remember a time in my life when I hadn't yet combined chocolate, tahini, and passionfruit. I am obsessed with each ingredient on its own, but the combination is mind-blowingly good. The slightly bitter dark chocolate goes amazingly well with the nutty, earthy tahini, while the tart passionfruit brings out the flavor notes of each. I often top this toast with crushed rose petals for a pop of beautiful pink.

1 slice **bread of your choice**

1 heaping tablespoon **tahini**

¼ cup **chopped dark chocolate (70% cacao or higher)**

1 tablespoon **maple syrup**

2 tablespoons **passionfruit pulp** (from 1 small passionfruit, see Tip, page 83)

Pinch of **sea salt**

½ teaspoon crushed **edible rose petals** (optional)

1 In a toaster or toaster oven, toast the bread to your preference.

2 In a small saucepan, combine the tahini, chocolate, and maple syrup over low to medium heat and cook, stirring frequently, for 2 to 3 minutes, until the chocolate is melted and the ingredients are fully combined. (If the mixture is too thick, add up to 1 teaspoon of water.)

3 Spread the chocolate-tahini mixture on the toast and top with the passionfruit and a small pinch of sea salt. Garnish with crushed rose petals, if desired.

unicorn toast

SERVES 2

Ah, Unicorn Toast, the toast that launched an Instagram phenomenon. Whether people loved it or hated it, this toast was suddenly everywhere. Using beet juice, I had been dyeing everything pink that I could get my hands on, including cream cheese. Then came the yellow-orange from turmeric, the light blue from spirulina, and the sea green from chlorophyll drops. When I arranged the colors on the toast, someone commented that the design looked like a unicorn, and the rest is history. Feel free to dress it up and top with your favorite fruit, hemp seeds, or granola!

2 slices bread of your choice

6 tablespoons cream cheese (I like nondairy)

3 teaspoons honey

1 teaspoon beet juice

½ teaspoon rosewater

½ teaspoon ground turmeric

½ teaspoon ground cinnamon

¼ teaspoon spirulina

TOPPINGS (OPTIONAL)

Pistachio Coconut Rose Dukkah (see page 33)

¼ teaspoon bee pollen

¼ teaspoon edible gold flakes

¼ teaspoon naturally dyed sprinkles

1 In a toaster, toast the bread to your preference.

2 In a small bowl, combine 2 tablespoons of the cream cheese and 1 teaspoon of the honey. Add the beet juice and rosewater, and mix with a spoon until fully blended and pink in color.

3 In a second small bowl, combine 2 more tablespoons of cream cheese and another teaspoon of honey with the turmeric and cinnamon, and mix with a spoon until fully blended and yellow in color.

4 In a third small bowl, combine the remaining 2 tablespoons cream cheese and 1 teaspoon honey with the spirulina, and mix with a spoon until fully blended and light bluish-green in color.

5 Put a dollop of each color on each piece of toast, then blend them using even knife strokes to make a pattern, then garnish with the Dukkah, bee pollen, gold flakes, and sprinkles, if desired.

mermaid toast

SERVES 2

Mermaid Toast is the blue and green cousin of Unicorn Toast. It's made up of naturally dyed cream cheese spreads: blue hues from spirulina and sea-green hues from chlorophyll. Mermaid Toast tastes best when it's topped with savory ingredients like the bagel seasoning and avocado. But if you prefer something sweet, you can add 1 teaspoon of honey when mixing each color and top the toast with shredded coconut or granola.

2 slices bread of your choice

4 tablespoons cream cheese (I like nondairy)

¼ teaspoon spirulina or blue majik

4 drops liquid chlorophyll

2 teaspoons Everything Bagel Seasoning, store-bought or homemade (see page 137)

½ avocado, sliced

1 teaspoon bee pollen (optional)

1 In a toaster or toaster oven, toast the bread to your preference.

2 In a small bowl, combine 2 tablespoons of the cream cheese with the spirulina and mix until fully blended and light blue in color. In a separate small bowl, combine the remaining 2 tablespoons cream cheese with the chlorophyll and mix until fully blended and green in color.

3 Spread the colored cream cheeses on the toast in a wave like stroke using a knife. Top with the seasoning, avocado slices, and bee pollen.

cactus toast

SERVES *1*

Cactus toast is probably the least practical way to eat kale, but it's definitely the most fun. Though this toast may look complicated, it's really quite the opposite. All you need is some hot pink cream cheese, a pair of scissors, and a desire to play with your food. Everything Bagel Seasoning adds a pop of flavor to this simple, cream cheese toast. Feel free to experiment with creating lots of different green plants on your toast.

1 slice **bread of your choice**

2 tablespoons **cream cheese (I like nondairy)**

1 teaspoon **beet juice**

1 leaf of **Tuscan/ lacinato kale**

Everything Bagel Seasoning, store-bought or homemade (see opposite), to taste

1 In a toaster or toaster oven, toast the bread to your preference.

2 In a small bowl, combine the cream cheese and the beet juice and mix until fully blended.

3 Using kitchen shears, cut one or two cactus shapes out of the kale and arrange on top of the toast. Top with Everything Bagel Seasoning to serve.

everything bagel seasoning

MAKES ABOUT ½ CUP

2 tablespoons sesame seeds

2 tablespoons poppy seeds

1 tablespoon dried minced onion

2 teaspoons dried minced garlic

2 teaspoons coarse sea salt

In a small bowl combine the sesame seeds, poppy seeds, onion, garlic, and salt in a small bowl. Store in an airtight container at room temperature for up to 6 months.

ab and h toast

SERVES 1

We're all well acquainted with PB and J, so I would like to introduce you to the AB and H: almond butter and honey. I like to use almond butter because it's rich with healthy fats and protein. Grapefruit zest adds a fun twist and pop of acidity to the rich flavors, but you can substitute lemon or orange zest if you don't have a grapefruit on hand. Pro tip: double-check that your almond butter is unsweetened, because this recipe calls for honey!

1 slice bread of your choice

1 tablespoon almond butter

1 or 2 fresh or dried figs, sliced

1 teaspoon hemp seeds

1 to 2 teaspoons pumpkin seeds

½ teaspoon honey

½ teaspoon grated grapefruit zest

1 In a toaster or toaster oven, toast the bread to your preference.

2 Spread the almond butter on the toast and top with the figs, hemp seeds, pumpkin seeds, a drizzle of honey, then sprinkle on the grapefruit zest.

turmeric egg toast

SERVES 2

My adoration for turmeric's vibrant yellow color and seemingly magical health properties knows no bounds. Turmeric is one of the most anti-inflammatory foods in the world, especially when combined with black pepper. The curcumin in turmeric gives the poached egg a vibrant yellow color and bold flavor that works perfectly with its savory flavor. Warning: you may never be able to go back to regular eggs again.

1 teaspoon **apple cider vinegar**

1 teaspoon **ground turmeric**

2 cups **water**

2 **medium eggs**

2 slices **bread of your choice**

1 **avocado**, sliced

1 **carrot**, shaved into ribbons

3 sprigs of fresh dill, or ½ teaspoon **dried dill**

Kosher salt and freshly ground black pepper, to taste

1 In a medium saucepan, bring the apple cider vinegar, turmeric, and water to a boil over high heat. Reduce the heat to medium-low and keep at a steady simmer. Crack one egg into a small dish or ramekin and then carefully add to the water, occasionally swirling and ladling water atop the egg to help it cook. Let the egg cook for about 5 minutes, remove with a slatted spoon, and place on a paper towel–lined plate. Repeat with the remaining egg.

2 In a toaster or toaster oven, toast the bread to your preference.

3 Top each piece of toast with some sliced avocado, carrot ribbons, and then a turmeric-poached egg. Sprinkle with the dill, and season to taste with salt and pepper.

eggplant toast, two ways

I was inspired to develop these eggplant toasts after getting well into the sweet potato toast lifestyle. Eggplant also makes a great toast base, as it's sturdy and holds up the flavors of a variety of toppings. Since the ever-versatile eggplant is often the star of my favorite Middle Eastern dishes, I decided to make sweet and savory versions using those flavors. Enjoy separately or together!

FOR THE EGGPLANT TOAST

1 medium to large Italian eggplant, sliced lengthwise into 6 pieces 1 inch thick

2 teaspoons extra-virgin olive oil

½ teaspoon ground sumac

½ teaspoon za'atar

½ teaspoon garlic powder

¼ teaspoon salt

Pinch of freshly ground black pepper

1 Preheat oven to 350°F and line a rimmed baking sheet with parchment paper.

2 Place the eggplant on the baking sheet and toss with the olive oil, sumac, za'atar, garlic powder, and salt and pepper. Roast for 25 to 30 minutes, or until the eggplant is fork-tender and lightly browned. Top with your preferred variation(s).

tahini and carrot eggplant toast

¼ cup tahini

⅓ cup Crunchy Chickpeas (see page 117)

1 large carrot, shaved into ribbons

Pinch of sea salt, to taste

Top each eggplant slice with tahini, chickpeas, carrot, and salt to taste.

pomegranate and mint eggplant toast

¼ cup cream cheese

2 teaspoons raw honey

¼ cup pomegranate seeds

¼ cup fresh mint leaves, chopped

Top each eggplant slice with cream cheese, raw honey, pomegranate seeds, and fresh mint.

plates

larb lettuce wraps

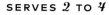

SERVES 2 TO 4

My family and I used to get Thai food from our favorite take-out spot at least once a week. We would always get larb, a brightly flavored, spicy ground meat salad with lots of fresh herbs. While this recipe is by no means a traditional larb, it's my way of satisfying that Thai food take-out craving. The preparation is ridiculously quick and easy—it's even faster than delivery. If you can find kelp noodles at your grocery store, give them a try here.

1 tablespoon avocado oil

1 large shallot, minced

1 garlic clove, minced

1 pound ground turkey or chicken

Pinch of sea salt

Juice of 2 limes (about 4 tablespoons)

3 tablespoons fish sauce

1 tablespoon coconut sugar

¼ teaspoon crushed red pepper flakes

½ red onion, thinly sliced

1 cup fresh basil leaves, finely chopped

1 cup fresh cilantro leaves, finely chopped

1 cup fresh mint leaves, finely chopped

2 tablespoons crushed peanuts

1 package kelp noodles (optional)

1 small head of butter or iceberg lettuce

1 In a large skillet, heat the avocado oil over medium high heat. When the oil is shimmering, add the shallot and garlic and cook for about 3 minutes or until translucent. Add the meat and salt and cook, breaking up the meat with a wooden spoon, until browned, 5 to 7 minutes.

2 In a small bowl, whisk together the lime juice, fish sauce, coconut sugar, and crushed red pepper flakes.

3 In a large bowl, combine the meat mixture with the onion, basil, cilantro, mint, and peanuts and combine with the sauce. If using kelp noodles, prepare them according to the package instructions and mix into the bowl. Let sit for at least 10 minutes to allow the flavors to meld.

4 Spoon the meat and noodle mixture onto lettuce leaves and enjoy. Store in an airtight container in the refrigerator for up to 5 days.

lentil burgers

These filling, vegetarian burgers are loaded with plant-based protein and healthy fats, and that's not even the best part. They're so versatile you can enjoy them on a traditional burger bun with ketchup and mustard, wrapped in a collard green or lettuce wrap, rolled into meatless meat balls and served with some pasta, or even crumbled over a salad. You can also customize the type of grains used in this recipe: I usually opt for brown rice, wild rice, or quinoa.

2 cups dried black lentils, cooked and drained

1 (15-ounce) can black beans, drained and rinsed

1 cup cooked grains of your choice

½ cup almond flour

½ cup oat flour

2 or 3 garlic cloves, minced

¼ cup chopped red onion

1 Chia Egg (recipe follows)

1 teaspoon ground cumin

¼ teaspoon cayenne

¼ teaspoon chipotle chile powder (optional)

½ teaspoon sea salt, or to taste

8 hamburger buns

1 In a food processor, puree the lentils and beans until a uniform paste forms. Transfer to a large bowl and add the grain, flours, garlic, red onion, Chia Egg, cumin, cayenne, chipotle powder (if using), and salt. Combine, using your hands, until thick, then let sit in the fridge for 30 minutes to 1 hour, until firm.

2 Preheat the oven to 375°F and line a baking sheet with parchment paper.

3 Form the mixture into 8 patties and space evenly on the baking sheet. Bake for 13 minutes, then flip and cook 13 minutes more, or until the burgers are firm and lightly browned.

4 Serve at once on the buns, with your favorite condiments. Store the burgers in an airtight container in the refrigerator for up to 1 week.

chia egg MAKES 1 EGG

1 tablespoon ground chia seeds

3 tablespoons filtered water

In a small bowl, combine the ground seeds and water, and whisk until fully blended. Let sit for at least 10 minutes or until gelatinous in texture, then use as an egg substitute in recipes.

sticky sumac salmon
with pomegranate chimichurri

SERVES *2*

Pomegranate and fish might sound like a strange pairing, but there's something seriously addictive about the combination of broiled salmon, fresh, garlicky chimichurri, and tart pomegranate taste that bursts in your mouth with every bite. I broil the salmon so that the coating of pomegranate molasses gets super-sticky and caramelized. You can find pomegranate molasses at any Middle Eastern grocery store or online. This salmon would be delicious atop the Tahini Honey-Mustard Kale Salad (see page 100).

2 garlic cloves, minced

1 teaspoon honey

2 teaspoons pomegranate molasses

¼ teaspoon ground sumac

Pinch of kosher salt

2 small pieces of salmon fillet (2 to 3 ounces each)

2 tablespoons Chimichurri Sauce (see page 175)

2 tablespoons pomegranate seeds

1 Preheat the broiler and line a baking sheet with parchment paper.

2 In a small bowl, combine the garlic, honey, molasses, sumac, and salt. Place the salmon pieces on the prepared baking sheet skin side down and coat with the mixture. Broil for 7 minutes, or until the salmon is opaque and flakes easily.

3 Combine the chimichurri with the pomegranate seeds and spoon on top of the salmon before serving.

paleo crispy
chicken sandwich

SERVES *2* TO *4*

Who doesn't love a crispy fried chicken sandwich? In the days before I was "vibrant" and "pure," you could regularly find me ordering a crispy chicken sandwich at a fast-food drive–through. Since that craving definitely stuck with me, I made this healthy version that is just as delicious and can be served on a grain-free bun or a lettuce or collard green wrap. The crispy chicken fillets are breaded in homemade grain-free crackers and baked instead of fried. Heads up: this recipe is best prepared the night before—but it's worth the wait!

4 (4-ounce) chicken breasts, cut in half (8 pieces total)

1 teaspoon garlic powder

½ teaspoon onion powder

1 teaspoon sweet paprika

½ teaspoon salt

⅛ teaspoon ground cayenne pepper

Pinch of freshly ground black pepper

2 tablespoons avocado oil

1 teaspoon apple cider vinegar

¼ cup pickle juice

½ teaspoon finely chopped fresh dill or 1 teaspoon dried dill

1 teaspoon hot sauce of your choice

1 teaspoon honey

30 Almond Chia Crackers (see page 188) or store-bought equivalent

⅓ cup tapioca flour

Pinch of sea salt

2 medium eggs

FOR THE SPECIAL SAUCE

3 tablespoons veganaise or mayonnaise

3 tablespoons hot sauce (I like Crystal)

½ teaspoon apple cider vinegar

1 tablespoon pickle juice

1 tablespoon minced pickle

Kosher salt and freshly ground black pepper, to taste

grain-free buns, lettuce, or collard greens for serving

2 tablespoons Quick Pickled Onions (see page 108, for garnish

1 avocado, sliced, for garnish

½ cup pickles, sliced, for garnish

1 In a large bowl or zip-top bag, combine

the chicken, garlic powder, onion powder, paprika, salt, cayenne, pepper, avocado oil, apple cider vinegar, pickle juice, dill, hot sauce, and honey. Let marinate in the fridge for at least 4 hours to overnight.

2 Preheat the oven to 350°F and line a baking sheet with parchment paper.

3 In a food processor, pulse the crackers until they form a powder or flour texture, and pour into a shallow bowl. In a second shallow bowl, combine the tapioca flour with a pinch of sea salt. In a third shallow bowl, whisk the eggs. Dredge each chicken breast first in the flour, then in the egg, and finally in the breadcrumbs. Space the chicken cutlets evenly on the baking sheet. Bake for 25 to 30 minutes or until golden and crispy on the outside.

4 Make the special sauce. In a small bowl, combine the veganaise, hot sauce, vinegar, pickle juice, and pickle and whisk until fully combined. Season with salt and pepper to taste.

5 Serve the crispy chicken on the buns. Top each with special sauce, pickled onions, avocado slices, and pickles.

falafel burgers

I wish I could say that the star of this recipe is the falafel burger, but really the falafel, which, don't get me wrong, is also delicious, is just a vessel for consuming garlic mayo, also known as toum. If you've ever had a quality falafel or shawarma sandwich, it was most likely topped with this white sauce that would terrify a vampire. If you don't like garlic, toum is not for you—you've been warned. These falafel burgers are super versatile, you can enjoy them on a lettuce wrap, gluten-free bun, or salad.

FOR THE BURGERS

2 shallots or ¼ a yellow onion, chopped (about ⅓ cup)

4 garlic cloves

⅓ cup parsley, chopped

1 teaspoon salt

1 teaspoon za'atar

1 (15-ounce) can of chickpeas, rinsed and drained

3 tablespoons sesame seeds

1 medium egg or Chia Egg (see page 152)

½ teaspoon ground cumin

⅛ teaspoon ground cayenne pepper, to taste

½ cup oat flour (see Tip)

3 to 5 Beet-Pickled Turnips, for garnish (recipe follows)

FOR THE GARLIC MAYO

½ cup veganaise or mayonnaise

4 garlic cloves, about 1 tablespoon, finely minced

Juice of 1 lemon, about 2 tablespoons lemon juice

Sea salt, to taste

1 Preheat oven to 350°F and line a baking sheet with parchment paper.

2 Make the burgers. In a food processor, combine the shallots and garlic and pulse until finely minced. Add the parsley, salt, and za'atar and pulse until the parsley is finely chopped. Add the chickpeas, sesame seeds, egg, cumin, and cayenne pepper and process until the chickpeas are smooth and pureed and all the ingredients are combined. Add the oat flour and process until a dough forms.

3 Using your hands, divide the dough into four even portions, form them into patties, and place them on the prepared baking sheet. Bake for 15 minutes, then flip, and bake for 15 more minutes, or until golden brown and lightly crispy on the outside.

4 Meanwhile, make the garlic mayo. In a small bowl, combine the vegannaise, garlic, lemon juice, and salt and whisk until fully combined.

5 Remove the burgers from the oven and let cool. Top with garlic mayo and beet-pickled turnips to serve.

tip: You can either buy oat flour at the store or make it yourself. Simply add oats to a blender or food processor and process until a flour forms.

beet-pickled turnips

MAKES *2* CUPS

½ cup rice vinegar

½ teaspoon sea salt

1 teaspoon coconut sugar

4 large turnips, peeled and cubed (about 2 cups)

1 small red beet, peeled and cubed

1 jalapeño, deseeded (optional)

1 In a medium saucepan, combine the rice vinegar, sea salt, coconut sugar, and 1½ cups water. Bring to a boil over high heat, then immediately reduce the heat and simmer for about 5 minutes, or until the sugar is fully dissolved.

2 Place the turnips, beets, and jalapeño in a 32-ounce jar. Pour the brine mixture over the vegetables, then let cool completely, about 30 minutes. Cover and store in the refrigerator for up to a month.

kabocha squash "mac and cheese"

Let's talk comfort food. When I discovered that certain foods caused my hormonal breakouts, I quickly saw my favorite foods flashing before my eyes—macaroni and cheese being one of them. The boxed type is often no more than powdered cheese and preservative-laden ingredients, but even when it's made fresh, a classic mac and cheese is basically a lot of glutinous pasta and dairy. This ridiculously creamy "cheese sauce" is actually made with squash that will quickly satisfy your comfort-food craving.

¼ kabocha squash, seeds removed

½ teaspoon avocado oil

½ teaspoon garlic powder

Kosher salt, to taste

1 teaspoon unsalted butter or coconut oil

1 medium onion, diced

4 garlic cloves, minced

1 teaspoon ground turmeric

¼ cup coconut milk (preferably culinary grade)

¼ cup nutritional yeast

2 tablespoons extra-virgin olive oil

1 teaspoon sweet paprika

½ teaspoon onion powder

⅛ teaspoon cayenne

Freshly ground black pepper, to taste

1 (8-ounce) box gluten-free pasta (I like red lentil pasta), preferably organic

1 Preheat the oven to 400°F and line a baking sheet with parchment paper.

2 Brush the squash with the avocado oil and sprinkle with the garlic powder and a pinch of salt. Place the squash flesh side down on the baking sheet and bake for 25 minutes, or until fork-tender. Let cool for 10 minutes.

3 In a medium skillet, melt the butter over medium heat. Add the onion, garlic, turmeric, and a pinch of salt. Sauté until the onion and garlic are translucent and soft, about 5 minutes.

4 Scoop out the flesh of the squash and place it in a high-speed blender or food processor. Add the coconut milk, nutritional yeast, olive oil, paprika, onion powder, and cayenne and blend until smooth and thick. Taste and add salt and pepper to your liking.

5 In a large saucepan, cook the pasta according to the package instructions. Drain the pasta and return it to the pot, then add the "cheese" sauce and stir to combine. Spoon the mac and cheese into bowls and enjoy!

roasted garlic chicken

SERVES 4

The truth is, you could turn on the oven, add some salt and pepper to a chicken, and roast it, and it will be darn near perfect. But I've got a few additions to take things up a notch. The green sauce that accompanies this chicken is inspired by a recipe my dad always has on hand—it's a little bit spicy and full of salty, herbaceous flavor. You can serve this sauce with literally anything, but it's especially good on this chicken. Add a green salad or some roasted veggies on the side.

1 whole chicken (about 6 pounds), preferably organic and pasture-raised

2 teaspoons salt

6 garlic cloves, minced

1 shallot, minced

¼ cup fresh parsley, minced

Grated zest of 1 lemon (about 1 tablespoon)

1 tablespoon extra-virgin olive oil

1 teaspoon red wine vinegar

½ teaspoon dried thyme

½ teaspoon dried rosemary

½ teaspoon sweet paprika

1 teaspoon freshly ground black pepper

⅓ cup Green Sauce (recipe follows)

1 Place the chicken in a roasting pan. In a small bowl, whisk together 1 teaspoon of the salt, the garlic, shallot, parsley, lemon zest, olive oil, vinegar, thyme, rosemary, paprika, and pepper. Rub the mixture onto the chicken, making sure to get some seasoning underneath the skin. Cover with plastic and let the chicken marinate for at least 1 hour in the refrigerator.

2 Preheat the oven to 425°F.

3 Roast the chicken for 45 minutes to 1 hour, or until the skin is crispy and browned and the temperature reaches 165°F on a meat thermometer. Remove from the oven and let cool.

4 Carve the chicken and serve with a generous dollop of Green Sauce on the side.

green sauce MAKES *1* CUP

4 garlic cloves

1 jalapeño pepper

1 (4-ounce) bunch of fresh cilantro (stems and leaves)

2 tablespoons extra-virgin olive oil

1 tablespoon pepperoncini brine (see Tip)

½ teaspoon salt

In a food processor, combine the garlic, jalapeño, and cilantro and pulse until finely chopped. Add the olive oil and brine and puree until a uniform green sauce forms. Use immediately or store in an airtight container in the refrigerator for up to 2 weeks.

tip: If you don't have pepperoncini brine, feel free to substitute pickle juice. If you don't have either, you can use white wine vinegar, but make sure to taste and adjust the salt, as pepperoncini and pickle juices provide extra saltiness.

roasted cauliflower tacos

If you're looking to get into meatless Mondays or you simply don't have any meat on hand, these roasted cauliflower tacos are exactly what you need. You carnivores out there might think it impossible to have an equally delicious veggie taco, but you'd be wrong. The roasted cauliflower florets are soft yet crunchy, and once they're tossed in sriracha-lime mayo, they are just as good as the more traditional pork, beef, chicken, and fish alternatives.

FOR THE SRIRACHA-LIME MAYO

¼ cup veganaise or mayonnaise

1 tablespoon sriracha

½ teaspoon chipotle chile powder

Juice of 1 lime (about 2 tablespoons)

2 garlic cloves, minced

12 corn tortillas

2 tablespoons Quick Pickled Onions (see page 108)

1 jalapeño pepper, sliced

½ cup chopped fresh cilantro

6 lime wedges

FOR THE CAULIFLOWER

1 cauliflower, cored and broken into bite-sized florets

1 tablespoon avocado oil or extra-virgin olive oil

1 teaspoon chipotle chile powder

1 teaspoon garlic powder

1 teaspoon onion powder

1 teaspoon sea salt

1 Preheat the oven to 425°F and line a rimmed baking sheet with parchment paper.

2 Make the cauliflower. On the baking sheet, toss the cauliflower with the avocado oil, chipotle, garlic powder, onion powder, and salt. Spread the cauliflower in an even layer and roast for 20 to 25 minutes, turning halfway through, or until lightly browned. Let cool for 10 minutes.

3 Make the sriracha-lime mayo. In a small bowl, whisk the veganaise, sriracha, chipotle, lime juice, and garlic until emulsified.

4 Transfer the roasted cauliflower to a medium bowl and add 2 to 3 tablespoons of the mayo. Toss vigorously to coat.

5 Divide the cauliflower among the the tortillas. Top each with some of the pickled onion, jalapeño, and cilantro. Drizzle with the remaining mayo and serve each with a lime wedge to squeeze over top.

coconut bolognese
with zucchini noodles

SERVES 4

Many years ago, I stumbled upon Marcella Hazan's famous bolognese recipe in the *New York Times*, and I set out to emulate this famous twist *sans* dairy. For this recipe, you can use any kind of ground meat you'd like, red or white wine, and any pasta your heart desires, though I typically serve it over zucchini (zoodles) or lentil noodles.

1 tablespoon unsalted butter or ghee

4 garlic cloves, minced

2 cups diced onions (2 medium onions)

1 teaspoon salt

1½ cups diced carrots (4 large carrots)

1½ cups diced celery (4 stalks)

1 pound ground beef

¼ teaspoon freshly ground black pepper

1 cup full-fat coconut milk (preferably culinary grade)

⅛ teaspoon grated nutmeg

1 cup dry wine

1 (28-ounce) can whole tomatoes, drained and crushed

1 tablespoon extra-virgin olive oil

Crushed red pepper flakes, to taste

4 medium zucchini

1 In a large skillet or Dutch oven, heat the butter, garlic, onions, and ½ teaspoon of the salt over medium heat and cook until the garlic and onions are softened and translucent, about 5 minutes. Add the carrots and celery and cook until softened, about 10 minutes more.

2 Increase the heat to medium-high and add the meat along with the pepper and remaining ½ teaspoon salt. Cook, breaking up the meat with a wooden spoon, until browned, about 10 minutes. Add the coconut milk and nutmeg and let simmer, stirring frequently, until the coconut milk has cooked down, 5 to 10 minutes. Then add the wine and let simmer about 30 minutes more.

3 Reduce the heat to low, add the tomatoes, and cook for 30 minutes to 1 hour, stirring occasionally. When you are ready to serve, drizzle in the olive oil and sprinkle with the red pepper flakes.

4 To make the zoodles, either use a spiralizer or simply grab a vegetable peeler and peel the zucchini into thin noodle-like strips. Heat the noodles in a skillet over medium heat for 5 minutes prior to serving.

grass-fed steak
with roasted cauliflower mash

SERVES 2

Whenever we have friends or family visiting, this is my go-to. It's a crowd pleaser and is really simple—plus, there's a lot you can do ahead of time so you won't spend all day in the kitchen. This cauliflower mash could turn a cauliflower hater into a believer, with its flavorful, fragrant roasted garlic and whipped, creamy texture. I recommend using skirt steak or flank steak for this recipe.

FOR THE CAULIFLOWER

1 cauliflower, cored and broken into florets

4 to 6 garlic cloves, unpeeled

2 tablespoons avocado oil

1 teaspoon garlic powder

½ teaspoon salt

4 teaspoons nutritional yeast

¼ teaspoon freshly ground black pepper

¾ cup full fat coconut milk

1 pound steak, preferably grass-fed

Kosher salt and freshly ground black pepper

1 tablespoon olive oil

¼ cup Chimichurri Sauce (recipe follows)

1 Preheat the oven to 400°F and line a baking sheet with parchment paper.

2 Make the cauliflower. Spread the cauliflower on the baking sheet along with the garlic. Toss with the avocado oil, garlic powder, and ¼ teaspoon of the salt to coat. Roast for 35 minutes. Let sit until the garlic is cool enough to handle. Squeeze the garlic out of their peels.

3 Place the cauliflower and garlic in a high-speed blender or food processor and add the remaining ¼ teaspoon salt, the nutritional yeast, black pepper, and coconut milk and blend until smooth.

4 Pat the steak dry and season with salt and pepper to taste. In a large cast-iron skillet or grill pan, heat the olive oil over medium-high heat. When it's shimmering, add the steak and sear for about 4 minutes, then flip and cook for 4 minutes more for medium-rare. Remove the steak from the skillet and let sit on a cutting board for 10 to 15 minutes.

5 Slice the meat across the grain. Divide the cauliflower between 2 plates, top each with slices of steak, and drizzle with the sauce.

chimichurri sauce
MAKES *1* CUP

4 garlic cloves

1 bunch fresh parsley

5 tablespoons extra-virgin olive oil

2 teaspoons white wine vinegar

½ teaspoon sea salt

¼ teaspoon crushed red pepper flakes

1 tablespoon pomegranate seeds **(optional)**

In a food processor, combine the garlic, parsley, olive oil, vinegar, salt, red pepper flakes, and pomegranate seeds (if using), and pulse until a thick chutney-like sauce forms. Use immediately or store in an airtight container in the refrigerator for up to 2 weeks.

snacks and sides

everything sweet potato fries

SERVES *2*

If you've never dipped fries in ranch dressing, you haven't lived. This used to be my favorite pastime, but if you go the traditional potato and ranch route, it's certainly not the healthiest habit. Thankfully, I found a way to have my fries-and-ranch and eat them too. Meet Japanese sweet potatoes! These crispy-on-the-outside, slightly caramelized, and fluffy-on-the-inside fries won't leave you feeling poorly or your skin on the fritz. It's a win-win! Top them with Everything Bagel Seasoning for added crunch.

2 large **sweet potatoes**, halved lengthwise and sliced vertically into fries

2 teaspoons **avocado oil**

1 teaspoon **garlic powder**

¼ teaspoon **sea salt**

2 teaspoons **Everything Bagel Seasoning**, store-bought or homemade (see page 137)

2 to 3 tablespoons **Dairy-Free Ranch Dressing** (recipe follows)

1 Preheat the oven to 400°F and line a baking sheet with parchment paper.

2 In a medium bowl, combine the sweet potatoe wedges, 1 teaspoon of the avocado oil, the garlic powder, and salt. Using your hands, toss until well coated. Transfer to the baking sheet, evenly distributing the sweet potato fries, and bake for 15 minutes. Flip the fries over and cook for 15 minutes more, or until browned and crispy. Let cool slightly.

3 Return the sweet potato wedges to the bowl and toss with the remaining teaspoon avocado oil until well coated. Sprinkle with the seasoning and serve with a side of Dairy-Free Ranch Dressing.

dairy-free ranch dressing

MAKES ¼ CUP

4 tablespoons veganaise or mayonnaise

1 teaspoon apple cider vinegar

1 teaspoon dried dill (2 teaspoons fresh dill)

1 teaspoon onion powder

1 teaspoon garlic powder

¼ teaspoon sea salt

In a small bowl, combine the veganaise, vinegar, dill, onion and garlic powder, and salt, and whisk until fully combined. Use immediately or store in an airtight container in the refrigerator for up to 1 week.

smashed sesame cucumber

When I'm hangry and the thought of having to wait even 20 minutes for something to boil or bake is too much to bear, I turn to this snack. It's so simple, yet ridiculously satisfying and flavorful. Salty, spicy, and toasty is the king of flavor combinations, especially when infused with refreshing cucumber and creamy avocado. Bonus: the healthy fat and fiber in the avocado will satisfy your hunger and keep you full for hours.

1 large **English cucumber, cubed and smashed**

2 large or 3 medium avocados, diced

1 shallot or ¼ red onion, thinly sliced

1 large or 2 small watermelon radishes, diced

2 teaspoons toasted sesame oil

2 teaspoons rice vinegar

1 tablespoon sesame seeds

½ teaspoon sea salt

Pinch of crushed red pepper flakes (optional)

In a medium bowl, combine the cucumber, avocados, shallot, watermelon radish, sesame oil, vinegar, sesame seeds, and salt and toss until coated. Add a pinch of crushed red pepper flakes, if desired. The salad is best if eaten right away, but can be stored in an airtight container in the refrigerator for up to 1 day.

"cheesy" spirulina stovetop popcorn

SERVES 4 TO 6

Discovering the magic of adding nutritional yeast and spirulina to my popcorn was truly a snack epiphany. Nutritional yeast is loaded with B vitamins, but more important, it has a super-cheesy, umami flavor. Spirulina is packed with plant-based protein, vitamins, and minerals, plus it has an earthy, salty taste. It's basically like eating cheddar popcorn with superfood benefits. If you've never made your own popcorn on the stove with avocado oil and sea salt, prepare to have your mind blown! If you ask me, it's the only (and healthiest) way to make popcorn.

4 tablespoons
avocado oil

1 cup popcorn
kernels

Sea salt, **to taste**

4 tablespoons
nutritional yeast

1 teaspoon
spirulina

1 In a large, heavy-bottomed saucepan, heat the avocado oil along with a few corn kernels over medium-high heat. Once the tester kernels pop, add the rest of the kernels and give the pan a shake to coat. Cover and increase the heat to high. Cook for 3 to 5 minutes, or until the popping starts to slow down significantly.

2 Once the popping slows down, remove from the heat immediately, pour the popped corn into a large bowl or large brown paper bag, and sprinkle with salt to taste, the nutritional yeast, and spirulina. Shake until evenly distributed.

3 The popcorn is best enjoyed while warm and fresh. Store any leftovers in an airtight container at room temperature for a few days.

sweet and savory roasted delicata squash

SERVES *2*

When I used to hear people describe some health foods as "like candy," my eyes rolled back so hard I nearly saw my brain. Now, I'm about to describe a piece of roasted squash as "like candy." But hear me out: naturally sweet delicata squash becomes somewhat caramelized and crispy when it's roasted. These sweet rings are so easy to whip up that they make an amazing appetizer when you're entertaining—no one will be able to stop eating them.

1 delicata squash, peeled

1 tablespoon ghee or unsalted butter

¼ teaspoon sea salt

¼ teaspoon ground cinnamon

¼ teaspoon garlic powder

1 tablespoon fresh parsley, minced (optional)

1 to 2 tablespoons Pistachio Coconut Rose Dukkah (see page 33, optional)

1 Preheat the oven to 375°F and line a baking sheet with parchment paper.

2 Cut the squash in half, spoon out the seeds, then cut into 1-inch-thick rings.

3 Place the squash on the baking sheet and add the ghee, salt, cinnamon, and garlic powder; toss to coat. Bake for 25 minutes or until fork-tender and slightly caramelized.

4 Top with parsley and dukkah if desired. Store them in an airtight container in the refrigerator for up to 3 days.

almond chia crackers

MAKES ABOUT *30* SMALL CRACKERS

These grain-free, vegan crackers are so good they almost started drama in my household. I made a batch to use in another recipe, and Arash saw the crackers sitting out and grabbed one, ate it, and exclaimed, "Wow! What are these!?" I told him not to eat any more crackers because I needed them. But even so, he snuck cracker after cracker into his mouth. Sometimes when something's *that* good, it's hard to follow the rules.

2 cups almond meal

2 Chia Eggs (see page 152)

½ teaspoon kosher salt

¼ teaspoon freshly ground black pepper

¼ teaspoon onion powder

¼ teaspoon garlic powder

Pinch of cayenne (optional)

1 Preheat the oven to 350°F and line a baking sheet with parchment paper.

2 In a medium bowl, combine the almond meal, chia eggs, salt, pepper, onion powder, garlic powder, and cayenne. Use your hands to mix until a uniform dough forms. Shape the dough into a disk and roll out as thin as possible on a sheet of parchment paper. Cut the dough into small squares (or whatever shape and size you'd like) and place them on the baking sheet, separating them slightly.

3 Bake for 12 minutes, then flip each cracker and bake for 10 to 12 minutes more, or until the crackers are hard and golden brown. If the crackers are soft in the middle, bake up to 5 minutes more, being careful that the edges don't start to burn. Let cool on a rack. Store in an airtight container at room temperature for up to 2 weeks.

caramelized pomegranate carrots

SERVES 4

I'm a fan of caramelizing pretty much anything, and carrots are no exception. The tartness and subtle sweetness from the pomegranate molasses and honey make these carrots taste more like dessert than vegetables. Once the slightly sticky and sweet carrots have cooled, sprinkle them with a hearty amount of dukkah for some added crunch and floral flavor.

1 tablespoon pomegranate molasses

1 tablespoon extra-virgin olive oil

½ teaspoon apple cider vinegar

½ teaspoon honey

½ teaspoon crushed red pepper flakes

¼ teaspoon sea salt

15 large carrots, peeled and halved or quartered crosswise

2 tablespoons Pistachio Coconut Rose Dukkah (see page 33, optional)

2 tablespoons pomegranate seeds

Chopped fresh parsley, to taste (optional)

1 Preheat the oven to 400°F and line a baking sheet with parchment paper.

2 In a large bowl, combine the molasses, olive oil, apple cider vinegar, honey, red pepper flakes, and salt, and whisk until fully combined. Add the carrots, then toss to coat. Spread the carrots evenly on the baking sheet.

3 Roast the carrots for 15 minutes, then turn and cook for 15 minutes more. Turn once more and cook for 15 minutes more, or until the carrots are fork-tender and caramelized.

4 While still slightly warm, sprinkle the carrots with the Pistachio Coconut Rose Dukkah, pomegranate seeds, and fresh parsley, if desired.

charred poblano and corn guacamole

Here is a jazzed-up guacamole for when you're feeling a little fancy and want to take your guac to the next level. Charred corn and poblano chiles sounds complicated, right? Wrong. You don't even need a grill; you can char these vegetables right in your oven. This special spin on guacamole is a hit served with a bowl of your favorite tortilla chips or on a crudités platter.

1 ear of corn, husked

½ teaspoon avocado oil

1 poblano chile

4 ripe avocados, halved, pitted, and peeled

½ cup finely chopped fresh cilantro

¼ cup finely diced red onion

4 garlic cloves, minced

Juice of ½ lime (about 1 tablespoon)

½ teaspoon sea salt

1 Preheat the oven to 400°F.

2 Coat the corn in the avocado oil and wrap in aluminum foil. Wrap the poblano pepper in a separate piece of aluminum foil and place the corn and the pepper directly onto the oven rack. Roast for 15 minutes, until tender, then remove from the oven, open the foil packet, and set the oven to the broil.

3 Return the corn and pepper to the oven and broil, turning every minute, until the pepper starts bubbling and looks charred and the corn kernels are browned all over, about 5 minutes. Remove from the oven and let cool, then slice the kernels off the cob and dice the charred poblano.

4 In a large bowl, combine the avocados, cilantro, red onion, garlic, lime juice, and sea salt. Mash the avocados with a fork to your preference. Add the corn and poblano and combine until evenly distributed. Serve immediately.

beet hummus

Some hummus aficionados might not call this "hummus" because it doesn't contain chickpeas. But whether you call it "beet hummus" or "delicious hot pink stuff," it's really good for dipping everything in, and that's all that matters. You can make this with such a huge variety of vegetables, raw or roasted, and limitless flavor profiles, depending what you're in the mood for. In my opinion, anything mixed with tahini and garlic is worth eating.

1 raw beet, peeled and diced

4 garlic cloves, peeled

Juice of 1 lemon (about 2 tablespoons)

⅓ cup tahini

⅓ cup extra-virgin olive oil

½ teaspoon salt

¼ teaspoon ground cumin

In a high-speed blender or food processor, combine the beet, garlic, and lemon juice and pulse until finely minced. Add the tahini, olive oil, salt, and cumin and puree until a smooth hot pink hummus forms. Store it in an airtight container in the refrigerator for up to four days.

marinated olives

If you've ever had unexpected guests pop over and needed a last-minute snack to serve, then this one's for you, you fancy host, you! Plus, there's plenty of room for experimentation. I use briney Kalamata and velvety Castelvetrano olives for a nice balance, but you can use any type of olives you like. Additionally, you can use regular almonds, your favorite nut, or leave them out entirely. If you don't have an orange on hand, try lemon zest instead.

⅓ cup **Kalamata olives**

⅓ cup **Castelvetrano olives**

2 **garlic cloves,** minced

1 teaspoon **red wine vinegar**

2 teaspoons **extra-virgin olive oil**

⅓ cup **Marcona almonds**

½ teaspoon fresh or dried **thyme**

½ teaspoon **orange zest**

In a medium bowl, combine the olives, garlic, red wine vinegar, olive oil, almonds, thyme, and orange zest. Let marinate for about 5 minutes before serving. Store in an airtight container in the refrigerator for up to 3 days.

crunchy nut and seed butter

MAKES *1½* CUPS

My motto with ingredients and flavor profiles is often "the more, the merrier," so when I decided to make a nut butter, I didn't want to leave out any nuts or seeds. The process of making your own nut butter takes some patience; you have to continuously scrape down the ingredients in the processor until a butter forms, but this crunchy, salty butter is worth the trouble. You can slather the stuff on just about anything, or just spoon it right out of the jar.

½ cup raw almonds

½ cup raw hazelnuts

½ cup raw walnuts

½ cup raw cashews

½ cup raw pumpkin seeds

½ cup raw sunflower seeds

½ teaspoon vanilla extract

¾ teaspoon sea salt

2 tablespoons flaxseeds

1 tablespoon chia seeds

1 Preheat the oven to 350°F and line a baking sheet with parchment paper.

2 Spread the nuts and seeds evenly on the baking sheet and toast for about 10 minutes, or until all are lightly golden brown and fragrant.

3 In a food processor, combine the toasted nuts and seeds and puree, occasionally scraping down the sides, until the fats start to emerge and a butter forms, 10 to 15 minutes. Add the vanilla and salt and puree until blended.

4 Transfer the mixture to a medium bowl and fold in the flax and chia seeds using a spoon or spatula. Transfer the nut butter to an airtight container. Store in an airtight container at room temperature for up to 1 month.

desserts

chocolate chip cookie dough

MAKES ABOUT *2* CUPS

If you don't have fond memories of sneaking a handful or two of raw cookie dough right from the mixing bowl as a child, I'm sorry to inform you that you missed out. The tubs of cookie dough my friends and I would eat with a spoon after school probably weren't intended to be eaten raw, but, lucky for you this dough is! Whether you make this recipe and simply store it in a jar in the fridge for a sweet snack or roll it into dough balls to carry with you for little bites of energy, this grain-free, refined sugar–free, dairy-free recipe will give you that cookie dough experience without all the stuff your body doesn't need.

1½ cups
almond flour

¼ cup
coconut flour

2 tablespoons
coconut oil, **melted**

2 tablespoons
almond butter

1 teaspoon
vanilla extract

2 tablespoons
maple syrup

¼ teaspoon
sea salt

⅓ cup
chocolate chips

1 to 2 tablespoons
nondairy milk, **as needed**

1 In a medium bowl, combine the flours, coconut oil, almond butter, vanilla, maple syrup, salt, and chocolate chips with a spoon until a dough forms. If the dough seems dry or crumbly, add up to 2 tablespoons of nondairy milk a teaspoon at a time, until a softer and stickier dough forms.

2 Transfer the mixture to a jar or roll into 1-inch balls. Store in an airtight container in the refrigerator or freezer for up to 3 months.

raw chocolate espresso and toasted hazelnut bars

MAKES *10* BARS

What I love about making raw desserts like this is that it's not really baking. All you need are the soaked cashews, a sweetener, and a fat to bind it all together when it freezes. Since there are no eggs involved, you can also safely taste as you go and adjust as needed. The cashew base doesn't have enough of an espresso taste for you? Add a little more. Not sweet enough? Add another tablespoon of maple syrup. Keep in mind that you will need to soak the cashews overnight before making this recipe.

2 cups Chocolate Chip Cookie Dough (see page 202)

2 cups raw cashews, soaked and drained (see Tip, page 46)

¼ cup water

⅓ cup coconut oil, melted

¼ cup plus 2 tablespoons maple syrup

4 tablespoons cacao powder

4 ounces espresso

1 teaspoon vanilla extract

⅛ teaspoon sea salt

½ cup chopped hazelnuts

1 Line a 9-inch square baking dish with parchment paper.

2 Press the cookie dough into the bottom of the dish and place in the freezer while you prepare the filling, about 15 minutes.

3 In a high-speed blender or food processor, combine the cashews, water, coconut oil, maple syrup, cacao powder, espresso, vanilla, and salt until the mixture is smooth. Taste and adjust flavors to your liking. Pour the batter into the baking dish and spread to evenly distribute.

4 In a small skillet, toast the hazelnuts over medium-high heat for about 3 minutes, or until they are fragrant and golden brown. Sprinkle the hazelnuts evenly over the filling and lightly press in. Return the dish to the freezer and chill for 6 hours to overnight.

5 To serve, let the bars sit for 10 minutes at room temperature before cutting. Store in an airtight container in the freezer for up to 1 month.

no-bake lemon honey blondies

MAKES 8 BARS

If lemon bars and blondies had a baby, it would be these dense, doughy bars. They are ridiculously easy to make, and take no more than 10 minutes. Plus, you can store them in the freezer for up to a month (but they're so good they probably won't last that long). Make sure you thoroughly stir your almond butter because if it's too oily, the batter will be too soft and sticky.

2 cups almond flour

⅓ cup almond butter

¼ cup honey

1½ tablespoons coconut oil, melted

⅛ teaspoon ground cinnamon

½ teaspoon vanilla extract

¼ teaspoon sea salt

2 teaspoons grated lemon zest (from 1 lemon)

Juice of 1 lemon (2 tablespoons)

¼ cup dark chocolate chips

1 Line an 8-inch square baking dish with parchment paper.

2 In a medium bowl, combine the almond flour, almond butter, honey, coconut oil, cinnamon, vanilla, salt, lemon zest, lemon juice, and chocolate chips, stirring with a spatula or your hands until a dough forms.

3 Press the dough into the baking dish, making sure it is evenly distributed. Chill in the freezer for 4 hours to overnight. Before serving, let them sit at room temperature for about 10 minutes to soften. Store in an airtight container in the freezer for up to 1 month.

pink peach cardamom ice cream
with broiled apricots

SERVES 2 TO 4

Dairy-free ice cream sometimes gets a bad rap, so for this delight based on coconut milk, I made sure there was plenty of flavor to go around. Keep in mind that this recipe requires time to chill overnight, so take this into account when you've got a hankering for this frozen delight.

2 peaches, pitted and diced (about 2 cups)

½ cup diced peeled raw beet (1 small beet)

1 cup frozen or fresh raspberries or strawberries

1 (15-ounce) can full-fat coconut milk (preferably culinary grade)

1 teaspoon ground cardamom

¼ cup honey

2 fresh apricots, halved and pitted

2 tablespoons chopped walnuts

1 In a medium saucepan, cook the peach over medium-high heat for 5 minutes, or until it starts to soften and smell fragrant. Let cool for 10 minutes, or until cool to the touch.

2 In a high-speed blender, combine the peach, beet, raspberries, and coconut milk, and pulse until completely smooth. Pour the mixture back into the saucepan and add the cardamom and honey. Stir to combine and cook on medium-high heat for 5 to 7 minutes, or until the honey has completely dissolved.

3 Let the mixture cool completely, then transfer to a medium bowl, cover, and chill in the refrigerator for 6 hours to overnight.

4 Pour the chilled mixture into an ice cream maker and churn according to the manufacturer's instructions. Remove the ice cream using a spatula and transfer to an airtight container to freeze completely, 2 to 3 hours.

5 When you are ready to serve the ice cream, preheat the broiler and line a baking sheet with parchment paper.

6 Place the apricot halves flesh-side down on the baking sheet and broil for 10 minutes, flipping half way through, until they are lightly browned and caramelized.

7 In a small skillet, toast the walnuts over medium-high heat for 3 to 5 minutes, or until fragrant and golden brown.

8 Scoop the ice cream into bowls and top with the walnuts and apricot.

blood orange–passionfruit cheesecake

MAKES ONE *9*-INCH CAKE

The first time I made a raw cashew cheesecake I was truly in shock. How in the world can this "nut cake" taste so much like cheesecake? All you need to do is blend raw, soaked cashews with melted coconut oil and a refined sugar-free sweetener, and then you can play around with as many fruits, herbs, and flavors you think of. If blood oranges aren't in season, feel free to use any other kind of orange or citrus fruit. Keep in mind that you will need to soak cashews overnight before making this recipe.

FOR THE CRUST

1 cup walnuts

½ cup hazelnuts

½ cup pitted dates

½ teaspoon vanilla extract

¼ teaspoon sea salt

FOR THE FILLING

2 cups raw cashews, soaked and drained (see Tip, page 46)

¼ cup coconut oil, melted

⅓ cup maple syrup

Juice of 1 blood orange (about ½ cup)

1 tablespoon grated lemon zest

Juice of 1 lemon (about 2 tablespoons)

2 tablespoons passionfruit pulp (from 1 passionfruit)

1 teaspoon vanilla extract

2 tablespoons diced peeled raw beet (optional)

1 Make the crust. In a food processor, combine the walnuts, hazelnuts, dates, vanilla, and salt until a thick and slightly sticky dough forms. Press the mixture into the bottom of a 9-inch springform pan and chill in the freezer, about 15 minutes.

2 Make the filling. In a high-speed blender, combine the cashews, coconut oil, maple syrup, orange juice, lemon zest, lemon juice, passionfruit pulp, vanilla, and beet and blend on high until smooth. Add up to 4 tablespoons of water, as needed, until smooth. Taste and adjust flavors to your liking.

3 Pour the filling over the crust and spread to evenly distribute. Return to the freezer and chill for 6 hours to overnight.

4 To serve, let cake sit at room temperature for at least 10 minutes. Store the cake in an airtight container in the freezer for up to a month.

toasted coconut butter fudge

My first memories of fudge are from Bethany Beach, Delaware. The boardwalk had all the best treats: fries with Old Bay and vinegar, funnel cakes, ice cream, and last, but certainly not least, fudge. I would get my pound of fudge, hide it from my family, and dig into my stash at every opportunity. This healthy twist on my favorite chocolate–peanut butter guilty pleasure uses toasted coconut butter as the filling. It's basically a superfood.

FOR THE TOASTED COCONUT BUTTER

3 cups unsweetened shredded coconut

2 teaspoons maple syrup

½ teaspoon vanilla extract

¼ teaspoon salt

FOR THE FUDGE

½ cup coconut oil

½ cup cacao powder

4 tablespoons maple syrup

½ cup smooth almond butter

Pinch of kosher salt

1 Preheat the oven to 350°F and line a baking sheet with parchment paper.

2 Make the toasted coconut butter. Spread the coconut on the baking sheet and toast for 7 to 10 minutes or until light brown.

3 In a food processor, pulse the coconut, occasionally scraping down the sides, until a butter-like consistency starts to form. Add up to 3 tablespoons of water as needed, then add the maple syrup, vanilla, and salt and pulse to combine. Scrape the coconut butter into a bowl and set aside.

4 Make the fudge. In a medium skillet, combine the coconut oil, cacao powder, maple syrup, almond butter, and salt over low heat, stirring frequently, until the coconut oil is melted. Pour half the mixture into a silicone ice tray. Layer ¼ teaspoon of coconut butter into each square, then top with the remaining fudge mixture so the coconut butter is fully covered. Chill in the freezer for at least 4 hours to overnight.

5 To serve, let the fudge sit at room temperature for 5 to 10 minutes. Store in an airtight container in the freezer for up to a month.

salted tahini walnut–chocolate chip cookies

MAKES *8* LARGE OR *16* SMALL COOKIES

I always shock people when I serve them these cookies and explain that they are both grain-free and vegan. These sweet and savory wonders will turn even your pickiest friends and healthy-eating naysayers into believers. They are crispy on the outside, gooey, moist, and dense on the inside, and layered with melty chocolate so every bite is like a little piece of salty-sweet heaven.

1½ cups almond flour

¼ cup coconut flour

¼ tapioca flour

1 teaspoon baking soda

1 teaspoon sea salt

⅓ cup coconut sugar

4 tablespoons coconut oil or butter, softened

3 tablespoons maple syrup

1 Chia Egg (see page 152)

1 teaspoon vanilla extract

6 tablespoons tahini (see Tip)

⅓ cup chopped walnuts

¼ cup dark chocolate chips

Pinch of flaky sea salt (I like Maldon)

1 Preheat the oven to 350°F and line a baking sheet with parchment paper.

2 In a medium bowl, combine the flours, baking soda, and salt.

3 In the bowl of a stand mixer fitted with the paddle attachment, combine the coconut sugar, coconut oil, and maple syrup and beat on medium to high speed about 30 seconds. Add the chia egg, vanilla, and tahini, and beat about 15 seconds more. Gradually add the flour mixture and beat until a dough forms. Fold in the walnuts and chocolate chips with a spatula until evenly distributed.

4 Portion out 1½ tablespoons of dough for small cookies or 3 tablespoons for large cookies. Roll the portions into balls, then flatten between your palms and place on the baking sheet 1½ to 2 inches apart. Sprinkle each with the flaky salt. Bake for 12 to 15 minutes, or until golden brown, and let cool on a rack. These cookies are best right out of the oven, but they can be stored in an airtight container at room temperature for up to a week.

tip: Try to avoid including any of the oil that comes with the tahini—just use the pure tahini. I dig underneath the layer of oil and carefully pour off any excess oil, though a small amount is okay.

chocolate-chunk walnut–banana bread doughnuts

MAKES *12* DOUGHNUTS

Who doesn't love doughnuts? Who doesn't love banana bread? Who wouldn't want to eat both at once without the sugar hangover? I'm a believer in "there's no such thing as too much of a good thing," so this one is for the dessert dreamers out there. The best part is that if you don't have a doughnut pan, this recipe also works as a sweet bread in a standard (9 by 5-inch) loaf pan, baked for 45 to 50 minutes.

4 ripe bananas

1 Chia Egg (see page 152)

¼ teaspoon vanilla extract

3 tablespoons maple syrup

1½ cups oat flour

1 cup almond flour

1 teaspoon baking powder

½ teaspoon baking soda

¼ teaspoon ground cinnamon

¼ teaspoon salt

⅓ cup chocolate chunks or chips

⅓ cup chopped walnuts

1 Preheat the oven to 350°F and coat two 6-cup doughnut pans with cooking spray.

2 In a medium bowl, mash the bananas using a fork until they are the consistency of applesauce, then stir in the chia egg, vanilla, and maple syrup.

3 In a large bowl, combine the flours, baking powder, baking soda, cinnamon, and salt. Add the banana mixture and mix until fully combined, then gently fold in the chocolate chunks and walnuts.

4 Spoon the batter into the doughnut wells, then bake each batch of 6 for 18 to 20 minutes, or until a toothpick inserted into the thickest part of a doughnut comes out clean. Remove the doughnuts from the pan and place on a wire rack to cool. Store in an airtight container at room temperature or in the fridge for up to 5 days.

acknowledgments

TO MY HUSBAND:
To my husband, Arash—you have been with me every single step of the way on this journey. You loved me at my McDonalds and caramel macchiato and you continue to love me at my lentil burger and matcha latte. From sitting in the old Toscana apartment brainstorming names for my new Instagram account to being my much needed taskmaster and forcing my procrastinating self to get all my recipes tested and finish my manuscript on time. You've dealt with my catastrophic messes in the kitchen and worked tirelessly (and oh so selflessly) as my recipe taste tester, and this cookbook would not be what it is without you. Thank you.

TO MJEAC
Thank you to my wonderful family. MJEAC is my mom's email address and it stands for all five of my family members' names. These four, my mother and father, brother and sister, mean the world to me and they have been my greatest supporters since the beginning. I thank my parents for trusting me to figure out what I was truly passionate about and encouraging me to follow through with it, though it felt scary at times.

TO MEG THOMPSON, MY AGENT
Dear Meg, quite simply—none of this would be possible without you! Thank you for seeing something in me and reaching out to me when you did. From the moment we first spoke on the phone, I wholeheartedly trusted you and your advice, and you've been easing my fears and going to battle for me ever since. I appreciate everything you've done for me and this book wouldn't be happening without you!

TO THE CLARKSON POTTER TEAM:
I am so grateful to everyone at Clarkson Potter who has helped to bring this book to life. Special thanks to my editors Amanda Englander and Gabrielle Van Tassel for working your magic. Thank you to the rest of the stellar team at Clarkson Potter, including Serena Wang, Jessica Heim, Stephanie Huntwork, Andrea Portanova, and Kristin Casemore.

TO DANIELLE DAITCH, MY RECIPE TESTER
Danielle: Thank you for being so very helpful and wise on this journey of developing recipes. Your experience and input was invaluable and these recipes would not be what they are without you!

TO MY VIBRANT & PURE COMMUNITY
To every single person who has shown an interest in what I am putting out into the world, this book is for you! Every kind comment and "like" still humbles me and I am forever honored to be able to inspire you to get creative with healthy food. Thank you!

Index

About the Author

Adeline Waugh is the creator of Vibrant &
Pure, a website and Instagram account that
celebrates merging the worlds of healthy
eating and innovative food styling. Adeline's
trendsetting work has been featured in *Vogue*,
Food & Wine, Refinery 29, the *New York Times*,
and more. Adeline currently lives in Miami,
Florida, with her husband, Arash.